Fearless Living

A 70 day reflective journey from fear to trust

Linda Knight

FIRST EDITION

ISBN: 978-1-939748-30-0

Library of Congress Control Number: 2013917234

Published by
NewBookPublishing.com, a division of Reliance Media, Inc.
515 Cooper Commerce Drive, #140, Apopka, FL 32703
NewBookPublishing.com

Printed in the United States of America

Disclaimer: The views and opinions expressed in this book are solely those of the authors and other contributors. These views and opinions do not necessarily represent those of New Book Publishing and Reliance Media Inc.

Dedication

To Marie (Skip) Brey and Deborah Thompson for
their faithful teaching of God's Word.

and

To my friend, Joan Pauls, for her love and support.

To a wonderful
woman of faith.
Take this adventure
one day at a time
~ & fearlessly

~ Charmaine

Table of Contents

Additional days to Encourage:

Introduction

This daily devotional study is a walk in learning not to live in fear. I was challenged by a speaker who said there were 365 references to *fear* in the Bible that were placed there to teach us how to handle fear appropriately, God's way. At the time, I was consumed by fear over circumstances in my life. To my surprise, I discovered there were more references in the Bible to fearing God than being instructed not to have fear in our lives. It began to seep into my thoughts that perhaps God wanted me to fear Him, not the circumstances of my life.

Fear, according to the dictionary, is defined as: being afraid, dread, frightened, anxious, doubtful, to have reverence or awe. God instructs us, with greater frequency, to have reverence and awe towards Him. We are to put our trust in Him rather than let fear consume us.

The desire to pursue a life without fear came after many experiences where I was terrified of my future. Surviving a divorce, raising two children and seeing them through college, struggling with my job and finances, losing my house, and going through bankruptcy all have produced a need for me to see things through God's perspective.

As you go through these passages, search for what God is asking you to give to Him so that you will not live in fear. He wants us to live for Him and to rejoice in our faith, trusting Him with our problems, worries and concerns. He is alive and well and more than able to defend, rescue, save, and comfort his faithful followers. Isaiah 49 is one of my favorite chapters as it holds many promises that help me during fearful times.

Isaiah 49:16 *See, I have engraved you on the palms of my hands; your walls are ever before me.* God knows me and won't forget me as I am engraved on His hands. He has my back and front. He is surrounding me!

Isaiah 49:23b *Then you will know that I am the LORD; those who hope in me will not be disappointed.* I need to learn about God and His character. Knowing God is essential to placing my hope in Him. He assures me that I will not be disappointed.

Isaiah 49:25b *I will contend with those who contend with you and your children I will save.* This verse gives me hope that God will do the contending (the battle is His) for me and for my children.

My desire is that you will find these daily study devotions a comfort and challenge. I pray that you will get to know our God better, seek His protection, and trust in Him daily. I also pray that you will gain strength and courage so you can lay your fears at His feet.

Linda Knight

How To Use This Devotion

1. **Pray before you start.**
2. Look up the passage in your Bible. The typed text is from the *New International Version* of the Bible (1984). <u>Read</u> the "do not fear" passage and context. The full text is noted if you have time to read the entire context of the "do not fear" passage.
3. <u>Meditate</u> on the verses and see if you are able to discern biblical truths. Biblical truths are distinguishing characteristics of God that are constant, always true and eternal.
4. <u>Read the Lessons and Truths</u> listed and see if you are able to add to this list.
5, <u>Pray</u> the prayer.
6. <u>Read</u> the passage that is listed for correctly placed fear.
7. <u>Do</u> the application questions and consider how you can apply the lessons and truths you have just studied in your life today!

One of the major purposes of studying God's Word is to get to know God better. Our trust and faith in God will be greater the more we know about His character. God desires that we become more and more like Jesus, so knowing God intimately is essential to our transformation. God's character is limitless so our study can be deep and lifelong.

2 Timothy 3:16-17 says, *"All scripture is God-breathed and is useful for teaching, rebuking, correcting and training in righteousness so that the man of God may be thoroughly equipped for every good work."* Each passage we study contains lessons that can be prayerfully meditated upon and applied to our lives.

As I completed this study, I learned many lessons about fear and how it has no place in my life if I am a follower of Jesus. I pray that this journey will help you to achieve *Fearless Living*, too.

Day 1–Genesis 15:1

Abraham's Shield

After this, the word of the LORD came to Abram in a vision:
> *"<u>Do not be afraid</u>, Abram.*
> *I am your shield,*
> *your very great reward."*

Context: God is speaking to Abram, later named Abraham, in a vision. He was getting older and knew he did not have any offspring (heirs). God wanted to refocus Abram so he would trust in Him alone for his future. Genesis 15:1-5

Lessons and Truths:
1. God is my protector and will defend me.
2. God is my reward in Himself and all things that come from Him are good for me.
3. With God as my shield, physically, emotionally and spiritually, I don't need to live a fear-filled life.
4. God knows me by name.

Prayer: Lord, help me to see You and Your shield and not the fearful situations that are surrounding me. Help me to look up to You for direction, guidance and to better realize that You are indeed my great reward. Help me to see that everything that comes from You is allowed by You and is good for me. Cause me to trust You more and more each day. Amen.

Well Placed Fear: Psalm 34: 7, 9

The angel of the Lord encamps around those who fear him, and he delivers them.

... Fear the LORD, you his saints, for those who fear him lack nothing.

How can I use these truths today?

What is happening to me that I can claim as goodness from God? _____

_____

_____

What fear do I need to give to God and ask for His strength and guidance? _____

_____

_____

Day 2-Genesis 21:17-19

Hagar's Rescue

God heard the boy crying, and the angel of God called to Hagar from heaven and said to her, "What is the matter, Hagar? <u>Do not be afraid</u>; God has heard the boy crying as he lies there. Lift the boy up and take him by the hand, for I will make him into a great nation." Then God opened her eyes and she saw a well of water. So she went and filled the skin with water and gave the boy a drink.

Context: Hagar and her son, Ishmael, were sent into the wilderness by Abraham due to conflicts with Sarah over Isaac's inheritance rights. Genesis 21:1-20

Lessons and Truths:
1. God cares about me and what distresses me. He is listening and watching.
2. God is sovereign and knows everything that goes on in my life.
3. God had plans for Ishmael's future just as he has plans for me.

4.   God shows mercy and compassion upon me.
5.   Fear comes from being overwhelmed and not reaching out to God.
6.   God can open my eyes to see His provision.

Prayer: Lord, help me to direct my pain toward You so that I may receive Your comfort and relief. Show me Your sovereign plan for my life and help me to trust You and walk with certainty knowing You are watching and listening for my cries for help. Amen.

Well-Placed Fear: Psalm 33:18-20

But the eyes of the LORD are on those who fear him, on those who hope is in his unfailing love, to deliver them from death and keep them alive in famine. We wait in hope for the LORD; he is our help and our shield.

How can I use these truths today?

What is threatening to overwhelm me with fear that I need to bring to the LORD? _____

_____

_____

God is listening and watching me. What do I need the LORD to specifically see and hear from me today? _____

_____

_____

Day 3-Genesis 26:24

Isaac's Reassurance

That night the LORD appeared to him and said, "I am the God of your father Abraham. <u>Do not be afraid</u>, for I am with you; I will bless you and will increase the number of your descendants for the sake of my servant Abraham."

Context: Isaac had just been embroiled in a 'well' controversy. He did not exercise faith in the situation and yet God favored him by allowing he and Rebekah to leave unharmed. He is also reminding him of his covenant and promises to Abraham and his descendants. Genesis 26:1-25

Lessons and Truths:
1. God is the same God that he was to my father, grandfather…. He does not change. He is immutable.
2. God promises to be with me in *all* situations.
3. All blessings come from God; I don't earn them by good behavior.
4. God has good things planned for my future.
5. God has the ability to bless generation to generation.

Prayer: Lord, help me trust You each day, in every situation and to expect blessings in my life and in the lives of those who come after me. Guide my children and grandchildren into Your ways, and let my life be an example to them of one who fully trusts in You. Amen.

Well-Placed Fear: Deuteronomy 5:29 and Proverbs 19:23

5:29 *Oh, that their hearts would be inclined to fear me and keep all my commands always, so that it might go well with them and their children forever!*

19:23 *The fear of the LORD leads to life: Then one rests content, untouched by trouble.*

How can I use these truths today?

In what situation do I need God today? _____

_____

_____

For whose future do I need to pray? Do they know the Lord?

_____

_____

_____

Day 4-Genesis 46:2-4

Israel's Coming Journey

And God spoke to Israel in a vision at night and said, "Jacob! Jacob!" "Here I am," he replied. "I am God, the God of your father," he said. "<u>Do not be afraid</u> to go down to Egypt, for I will make you into a great nation there. I will go down to Egypt with you, and I will surely bring you back again. And Joseph's own hand will close your eyes."

Context: This vision occurred during the famine years and Israel (Jacob) had just learned that his son Joseph was still alive and would provide for them in Egypt. Genesis 46:1-7

<u>Lessons and Truths:</u>

1. God can and does speak to me especially through His Word and prayer.
2. God does not want me to be afraid of the future.
3. Just like Jacob, I can have a history with God and can trust Him.
4. God has a plan for my life.

5. God can and does direct my path so fear of the future does not come from Him.

6. God goes before me and will protect me.

Prayer: Lord, slow me down so I can listen to You. Take my fears away and replace them with Your reassurance and comfort. Help me to trust You for my future and depend upon Your guidance. Amen.

Well-Placed Fear: Psalm 31:19

How great is your goodness, which you have stored up for those who fear you, which you bestow in the sight of men on those who take refuge in you.

How can you use these truths today?

What frightens you that you need to give to God? _____

_____

_____

Where do you need God to go before you today? ...this week? ...this month? _____

_____

_____

Day 5–Genesis 50:19-21

God's Good Intentions

But Joseph said to them, "Don't be afraid. Am I in the place of God? You intended to harm me, but God intended it for good to accomplish what is now being done, the saving of many lives. So then, don't be afraid. I will provide for you and your children." And he assured them and spoke kindly to them.

Context: Joseph's brothers feared him as they had sold him into slavery as a young man. With the death of their father Jacob (Israel), they feared Joseph would seek revenge. Genesis 50:15-21

Lessons and Truths:
1. Man may intend harm to me, but God's intentions are for my ultimate good.
2. God wants good things for me.
3. God is sovereign and directs actions to bring me good.
4. The will of God will not be thwarted.
5. God's will always sees to my provision.

Prayer: Father, help me to see things through Your eyes and look for ways that I can be conformed to Your will. Give me strength to face adversity and hope through trusting in You and Your provision. Amen.

Well-Placed Fear: Proverbs 22:4

Humility and the _fear_ of the LORD bring wealth and honor and life.

How can I use these truths today?

What is happening in my life that I need to pray and leave in God's hands?_____

_____

_____

_____

_____

Day 6-Exodus 14:13-14

God's Deliverance

Moses answered the people "Do not be afraid. Stand firm and you will see the deliverance the LORD will bring you today. The Egyptians you see today you will never see again. The LORD will fight for you; you need only be still."

Context: The Israelites were terrified as Pharaoh and his army were chasing after them. They were up against the Red Sea with no place to go. Exodus 14:5-31

Lessons and Truths:
1. In a crisis, the Lord wants me to be rooted, standing firm in faith.
2. I am to watch for His deliverance. I don't create deliverance; He brings it.
3. When God solves a problem, He does it completely. He has eternal answers.
4. God does the fighting, not me.
5. Patience and faith are required in God's battles.

Prayer: Lord, help me to stand firm in my faith awaiting Your deliverance. Open my eyes that I may see Your work and not try to solve the problem myself. Thank you for fighting for me. I know the battle is Yours. By Your grace, give me the patience and full measure of faith I need to bring You glory and honor. Amen.

Well-Placed Fear: Exodus 14:31

And when the Israelites saw the great power the LORD displayed against the Egyptians, the people <u>feared the LORD</u> and put their trust in him and in Moses his servant.

How can I use these truths today?

Where do I need to stand firm and watch for God's deliverance?

_____

_____

_____

Where am I struggling with waiting for God's solutions?

_____

_____

_____

Ask Him for an extra measure of patience today.

Day 7-Exodus 20:20

Moses Reassures Israelites

*M*oses said to the people, "<u>Do not be afraid</u>. God has come to test you, so that the fear of God will be with you to keep you from sinning."

Context: Moses will be meeting with God on the mountain and the people are afraid. He is trying to reassure them of God's purpose. Exodus 20:18-21

Lessons and Truths:

1.   God reveals himself to me to edify and build my faith.
2.   Only God is powerful enough to stop sin.
3.   Only the fear/awe of God will keep me on the right path in life.
4.   Trusting God is the only way to success.

Prayer: Lord, help me to trust You each day to direct my path and keep me from sin. Lead me in Your way that my life may glorify You in words and deeds. Amen.

Well-Placed Fear: Psalm 111:10

The _fear_ of the LORD is the beginning of wisdom; all who follow his precepts have good understanding. To him belongs eternal praise.

How can I use these truths today?

What sin do I need to surrender to Him? _____

_____

_____

Where do I need to trust Him today? _____

_____

_____

Day 8–Numbers 14:9

Joshua and Caleb Plead

"*Only do not rebel against the LORD. And <u>do not be afraid</u> of the people of the land, because we will swallow them up. Their protection is gone, but the LORD is with us. <u>Do not be afraid of them</u>.*"

Context: The spies had just returned with a report about the giants in the land and the people were grumbling that they should have stayed in Egypt. Moses and Aaron fell face down, while Joshua and Caleb pleaded with the Israelites to move forward and trust God. Numbers 13:26-14:9.

Lessons and Truths:

1.   I do not need to fear anyone or anything. God, who indwells me as a believer, is greater than anyone or anything I could ever face.
2.   My protection is from the LORD.
3.   My protection is greater than any that exists on Earth.
4.   God's presence with me insures that I will be victorious when doing as He requires.

5. God's enemies do not have his protection.
6. Walking with the Lord requires trusting Him for all my needs.
7. God's plan leads to victory, not defeat.

Prayer: Lord, help me to trust You and walk in Your ways. Help me to lean on You for protection, and that You will continue to be my shield, rock and salvation. Give me courage to face my enemies and persevere until victory is at hand. Amen.

Well-Placed Fear: Psalm 115:1

You who fear him, trust in the LORD- he is their help and shield.

How can I use these truths today?

These are my fears: _____

_____

_____

Is any greater than God? _____

_____

What fear can I entrust to God right now? _____

_____

_____

Day 9-Numbers 21:34

God Desires Victory

The LORD said to Moses, "Do not be afraid of him, for I have handed him over to you, with his whole army and his land. Do to him what you did to Sihon king of the Amorites, who reigned in Hesbon."

Context: As the Israelites were moving towards Canaan, they were passing through lands controlled by others. They defeated the Amorites and briefly settled there. Their next foe was Og king of Bashan, and God encourages the Israelites to be courageous and trust Him for victory. Numbers 21:21-35.

Lessons and Truths:
1. God has a plan that is bigger than my enemies.
2. My enemies are unaware (or underestimate, disbelieve) of the power and might of the Almighty God.
3. God's plan is for victory and not defeat. His way will lead to victory.
4. Fear is counterproductive and shows a lack of faith on my part and lack of trust in God's plans for my life.

5.   God wants me to completely defeat my enemies, eliminating the threat of them regaining a foothold in my life. My enemies can be things like unbelief, idolatry, depression, addiction, sexual sins, lack of forgiveness, and anger.

Prayer: Father, I lay my enemies (name them specifically) at Your feet. I know Your plan is for victory in my life. Take hold of these that have a grip on me and break those bonds freeing me by Your power so I can live a life trusting fully in You. Help me to believe in You and the victory You promise in my life. Amen.

Well-Placed Fear: Psalm 25:12

Who, then, is the man that fears the LORD? He will instruct him in the way chosen for him.

How can I use these truths today?

What enemies do I need to surrender to God so that I can live a life of victory in Him?_____

_____

_____

How will I let the LORD instruct me so that I can conquer my fears?

I will commit to study His Word daily _____

I will commit to praying for His guidance _____

I will _____

Day 10-Deuteronomy 1:20-21

Moses Sends Spies

Then I said to you, "You have reached the hill country of the Amorites, which the LORD our God is giving us. See, the LORD your God has given you the land. Go up and take possession of it as the LORD, the God of your fathers, told you. <u>Do not be afraid; do not be discouraged."</u>

Context: Moses was speaking to the people of Israel reminding them of God's command to go up and possess the land. After this, he chose 12 spies to go into the land and explore. Deuteronomy 1:19-25

Lessons and Truths:
1.   God gives direction to believers.
2.   God gives power to complete the work He intends for me to do.
3.   When I am following His direction, I do not need to be afraid or discouraged.
4.   No matter what it looks like ahead, I need to trust God and press onward.

5. Discouragement and fear are Satan's tools to stop my progress and work for the Lord.
6. God is more powerful than any enemy I can face.

Prayer: Father, give me clear direction as to what and where You want me to go in life. Help me to discern Your way correctly and step out in faith to follow You. Let me put my wants and desires aside and look for Your way in my life. Guard my way from discouragement and bind Satan from attacking and hindering the work You have given me to do. Amen.

Well-Placed Fear: Psalm 25:14

The LORD confides in those who fear him; he makes his covenant known to them.

How can I use these truths today?

To what work is God calling you? _____

_____

_____

I will seek God's direction in my life by_____

_____

_____

Day 11-Deuteronomy 1:29-31

God Carries Me

Then I said to you, "Do not be terrified; do not be afraid of them. The LORD your God, who is going before you, will fight for you, as he did for you in Egypt, before your very eyes, and in the desert. There you saw how the LORD your God carried you, as a father carries his son, all the way you went until you reached this place."

Context: Moses was reminding the Israelites of their parents' rebelliousness towards God when they refused to enter the Promised Land. Their sin cost them 40 years of desert wandering and death in the wilderness. Moses warns the new generation to trust God. Deuteronomy 1:26-46

Lessons and Truths:
1. With God, I do not need to fear men as God is greater than anyone or anything.
2. God goes ahead of me.
3. God promises He will contend (fight) for me.

4.   I need to *remember* how God has been with me and 'carried' me in times of trouble and distress. Therefore, I can trust Him with today's problems.

5.   God has a destination (place, purpose) in mind for me.

Prayer: Lord, help me to remember how You have upheld me in the past. Remind me of Your character, that You are immutable – the same yesterday, today and forever. I can count on You to help me today. Thank you for going ahead of me and having a place for me. I know You are faithful and I can depend upon You. Amen.

Well-Placed Fear: Philippians 2:12-13

Therefore, my dear friends, as you have always obeyed— not only in my presence, but now much more in my absence— continue to work out your salvation <u>with fear and</u> <u>trembling, for it is God who works in you to will and to act according to his good purpose.</u>

How can I use these truths today?

Remember a time of God's faithfulness to you. _____

_____

_____

What battle do I need God to fight for me today? _____

_____

_____

Day 12-Deuteronomy 3:2

Lord Handles Enemies

The LORD said to me, "<u>Do not be afraid of him</u>, for I have handed him over to you with his whole army and his land. Do to him what you did to Sihon king of the Amorites, who reigned in Hesbon."

Context: Moses and the Israelites are confronted by Og king of Bashan and his whole army as they make their way towards Canaan, the Promised Land. Deuteronomy 3:1-11.

Lessons and Truths:

1. The LORD knows the outcome of the battle before it even starts. He is always the winner.
2. The LORD will fight my battles for me, using His winning strategies, weapons, timing and soldiers, but I need to allow Him to fight for me. I can't decide to take the battle into my own hands and think I will win.
3. The LORD has handled my enemies in the past and will continue to do so in the future; I only need to trust Him.

4. The outcome of the battle was to be victory, defeat of the enemy, and then more than they expected – his land. I, too, will get more than expected if I trust God.
5. God expects me to follow His directions completely to achieve victory.
6. Fear comes from not trusting God.

Prayer: Lord, give me the faith I need to submit my battles to You. Thank you that You have a winning strategy to vanquish all my foes if I will only trust in You. Increase my faith as I leave the victory to You without fear. Amen.

Well-Placed Fear: 2 Kings 17:39

Rather, worship (fear) the LORD your God; it is he who will deliver you from the hand of all your enemies."

How can I use these truths today?

Lord, I am facing these battles in my life and I lay them before you. _____

_____

_____

_____

I trust you to win these battles. Help me to not take them back up again! Amen.

God Fights for Me

At that time I commanded Joshua: "You have seen with your own eyes all that the LORD your God has done to these two kings. The LORD will do the same to all the kingdoms over there where you are going. <u>Do not be afraid of them</u>; the LORD your God himself will fight for you".

Context: Moses was preparing the Israelites, by reviewing their history, just as they are preparing to enter the Promised Land. Moses would not be going with them due to his sin at Meribah (Numbers 20: 2-13). God allowed him to see the land from the top of Mt. Pisgah, then told him to commission Joshua and encourage him. Deuteronomy 3:21-29

Lessons and Truths:

1.   I can see evidence of God's victory in my life, but I have to ***look*** for it. I also have to remember what God has done for me in the past.

2.   God will contend with those who contend with me. This is a promise given in Isaiah 49: 25b. "*I will contend with*

those who contend with you and your children will be saved."

3.   God will fight my battles; He will not send a substitute.
4.   The God of the universe is my warrior.
5.   Fear comes from not trusting God to fight for me and doubting the outcome of the battle.

Prayer: Lord Almighty, great beyond measure, help me to trust You in the battles that are present in my life. Help me to believe in faith that You are stronger and mightier than any battle that can present itself in my life. You are my warrior. The battle is Yours so help me to live and act believing that You are and will always be victorious. Amen.

Well-Placed Fear: Psalm 27:1, 3

The LORD is my light and my salvation-whom shall I <u>*fear*</u>*? The LORD is the stronghold of my life- of whom shall I be afraid?..... Though an army besiege me, my heart will not <u>fear</u>, though war break out against me, even then will I be confident.*

How can I use these truths today?

What victories has God given me in my life that give me HOPE?

_____

_____

What battle can I lift up to God?_____

_____

_____

Day 14-Deuteronomy 18:21-22

Discerning Truth

You may say to yourselves, "How can we know when a message has not been spoken by the LORD?" If what a prophet proclaims in the name of the LORD does not take place or come true, that is a message the LORD has not spoken. That prophet has spoken presumptuously. <u>Do not be afraid of him.</u>

Context: Moses is instructing the people on how to test whether or not someone is a true prophet and speaking a message from God. Deuteronomy 18:14-22

Lessons and Truths:

1. Valid messages from God come true.
2. I must listen and watch with discernment to those who speak about God and His Word.
3. I must test what people say against God's Word as God's truth does not change. John gives further instructions in 1 John 4:1-3a.

      Dear friends, do not believe every spirit, but test the spirits to see whether they are from God, because many false prophets have gone out into the world. This is how you can recognize the Spirit of God: Every spirit that acknowledges that Jesus Christ has come in the flesh is from God. but every spirit that does not acknowledge Jesus is not from God.

Prayer: Lord, help me to rely on Your Word to guide me in discerning those that would seek to distort Your truth about Jesus. Give me a hunger for Your Word that I may grow and be grounded in Your truth so that I can stand firm in faith. Help me to use Your Word as a sword to thwart the enemy's attacks. Amen.

Well-Placed Fear: Psalm 119:33, 37-38

Teach me, O LORD, to follow your decrees; then I will keep them to the end....Turn my eyes away from worthless things; preserve my life according to your word. Fulfill your promise to your servant, so that you may be <u>feared</u>.

How can I use these truths today?

What have I heard recently that needs to be measured by God's word?_____

_____

_____

How will measuring what I hear against God's Word bring me assurance? _____

_____

Look these up for assurance: Psalm 119:138, 160; 2 Timothy 3:16-17.

Battle Attitude

When *you go to war against your enemies and see* *horses and chariots and an army greater than yours, do not be* *afraid of them, because the LORD your God, who brought you* *up out of Egypt will be with you. When you are about to go* *into battle, the priest shall come forward and address the army.* *He shall say: 'Hear, O Israel, today you are going into battle* *against your enemies. Do not be fainthearted or afraid; do not* *be terrified or give way to panic before them. For the LORD* *your God is the one who goes with you to fight for you against* *your enemies to give you victory."*

Context: Moses was addressing the children of Israel before they embarked on the conquest of Canaan. Deuteronomy 20:1-4

Lessons and Truths:
1. God knows all my adversaries.
2. Fear produces indecision and lack of conviction, something God does not want for me when I am in a battle.

3. Fear produces terror and can lead to panic which reduces my ability to reason and think.
4. God goes with me wherever my battle is located.
5. God goes with me to do the fighting.
6. Victories that come to me are through God's power.
7. God knows the day and time of each of my battles; they are not a surprise to Him. He wants me to be prepared and ready to stand firm.

Prayer: Lord, You know the battles that I am facing today, those I faced yesterday and will face tomorrow. Prepare me and help me to stand firm not being afraid or fainthearted. Help me to trust in You for the victory and give You all the glory! Amen.

Well-Placed Fear: Psalm 56:3-4

When I am afraid, I will trust in you. In God, whose word I praise, in God I trust; I will not be afraid. What can mortal man do to me?

How can I use these truths today?

When the decision about_____comes today or tomorrow, I will not be fearful, but will give it to God.

God, these are my adversaries: _____

_____

_____

Prepare me for battle and help me to recognize adversaries in my life, so that I will be able to stand firm and not be surprised.

Day 16-Deuteronomy 31:6-8

God's Faithful Presence

Be strong and courageous. <u>Do not be afraid or terrified</u> because of them, for the LORD your God goes with you; he will never leave your nor forsake you.

Then Moses summoned Joshua and said to him in the presence of all Israel, "Be strong and courageous, for you must go with this people into the land that the LORD swore to their forefathers to give them, and you must divide it among them as their inheritance. The LORD himself goes before you and will be with you; he will never leave you nor forsake you. <u>Do not be afraid; do not be discouraged</u>."

Context: Moses was speaking to all Israel and Joshua, God's chosen successor, as they are about to enter the promised land of Canaan after 40 years in the wilderness. Deuteronomy 31:1-8

Lessons and Truths:

1. God is strong and His strength can give me strength and courage.
2. God is omnipresent. He is always with me.

3. God is faithful. He is tenacious in sticking to me like no other and will never leave.

4. God desires for me to be courageous in actions and thoughts.

5. God has a job for me to do and it requires me to trust Him, putting my fears behind me.

6. God goes before me; He knows what lies ahead.

Prayer: Lord give me Your courage and strength. Keep terror and fear away from me. Put a shield around my thoughts to guard against fears. Help me to focus on You, rely on Your presence and accomplish what You have for me to do. Amen.

Well-Placed Fear: Proverbs 1:33

but whoever listens to me will live in safety and be at ease, without fear of harm.

How can I use these truths today?

I have these things coming up_____

_____and I need You to go before me to prepare the way.

What thoughts do I need to have protected by God so that I will not worry? _____

_____

_____

_____

Day 17-Joshua 1:8-9

His Word 24/7

"*Do not let this Book of the Law depart from your mouth; meditate on it day and night, so that you may be careful to do everything written in it. Then you will be prosperous and successful. Have I not commanded you? <u>Be strong and courageous</u>. <u>Do not be terrified; do not be discouraged</u>, for the LORD your God will be with you wherever you go.*"

Context: After Moses' death, the LORD spoke to Joshua. He gave him instructions and encouragement prior to leading the Israelites into the Promised Land. The Lord knew that Joshua was up to the task if he would focus on Him and his promises. Joshua 1:1-9

Lessons and Truths:

1. Following God's way requires attention 24/7 (day and night) to content and details of His Word.
2. Prosperity and success result in following God's Word.
3. God commands me to not be fearful or discouraged.
4. God's way demands that I trust Him.

5. God longs for me to know his presence daily wherever I am.

Prayer: Lord, You promise to be with me each day and speak to me through Your Word. Give me a desire to study Your Word and get to know You. Help me to trust You daily and depend upon Your presence in my life. Protect me from Satan's attacks that bring on fear and help me to look to You for guidance and success each day. Amen.

Well-Placed Fear: Proverbs 9:10-12a

"The fear of the LORD is the beginning of wisdom, and knowledge of the Holy One is understanding. For through me your days will be many, and years will be added to your life. If you are wise, your wisdom will reward you."

How can I use these truths today?

What am I doing each week to get to know God and His Word better? _____

_____

_____

What is causing me fear or discouragement in my daily walk with God that I need to give to Him? _____

_____

_____

Pray now and relinquish these worries to Him. Amen.

Day 18–Joshua 8:1

Grasping Victory God's Way

Then the LORD said to Joshua, "<u>Do not be afraid; do not be discouraged</u>. Take the whole army with you and go up and attack Ai. For I have delivered into your hands the king of Ai, his people, his city and his land."

Context: The Israelites were defeated at Ai because of their sin against God. Joshua was told to find out who had sinned and deal with them. Joshua did this, and then God sent them against the king of Ai again. Joshua 7-8:29

Lessons and Truths:

1. God has detailed plans for victory and they need to be followed.
2. God's victory is never small but total and all encompassing.
3. Following God's plan requires faith, trust and lack of fear.
4. God knows the outcome of the battle before it has even begun, so I need to take what God gives me and use it

while I trust in Him. NO FEAR!

5. God wants me to be victorious.

Prayer: Lord, increase my faith and help me to see Your plans clearly and follow them implicitly, trusting You for the total victory. Help me to trust You and not let doubt and fear creep into my mind. Put a hedge of protection around me to guard against Satan's attack. Amen.

Well-Placed Fear: Psalm 86:11-13

Teach me your way, O LORD and I will walk in your truth; give me an undivided heart, that I may fear your name. I will praise you , O Lord my God with all my heart; I will glorify your name forever. For great is your love toward me; you have delivered me from the depths of the grave.

How can I use these truths today?

Where does God want me to have victory in my life?

_____

_____

What is God asking me to do? _____

_____

_____

How can I praise and glorify God in this? _____

_____

_____

Day 19–Joshua 10:8

Assured Victory

*T*he LORD *said to Joshua, "<u>Do not be afraid of them</u>; I have given them into your hand. Not one of them will be able to withstand you."*

Context: Joshua had made peace with a city called Gibeon. Five surrounding kings then banded together to attack Gibeon because of their peace with the Israelites. The Gibeonites called Joshua to come quickly and save them. Joshua 10:1-15

Lessons and Truths:
1. God is sovereign and knows the end of the battle before I even begin.
2. God's plan is for victory, not defeat.
3. God is more powerful (omnipotent) than any of my enemies.
4. With God, NO ONE can stand against me when I am fighting His battle.
5. Joshua needed to trust God for the victory. I need to

entrust God with my battles and claim the victory in His name.

Prayer: Lord, help me to trust You with the battles in my life. Strengthen my faith so that I will stay strong in the battle and be assured of the outcome of victory. Take down my enemies that I might prevail and glorify You in the victory to come. Amen.

Well-Placed Fear: Proverbs 14:27 and Proverbs 29:25

14:27   The fear of the LORD is a fountain of life, turning a man from the snares of death.

29:25 Fear of man will prove to be a snare, but whoever trusts in the LORD is kept safe.

How can I use these truths today?

Where is God asking me to take a stand and entrust the outcome to Him? _____

_____

_____

What things are creating fear in my heart that I need to give to Him? _____

_____

_____

Pray right now and claim the victory in His Name!

Day 20-Judges 6:21-23

God's Peace

With the tip of the staff that was in his hand, the angel of the LORD touched the meat and the unleavened bread. Fire flared from the rock, consuming the meat and the bread. And the angel of the LORD disappeared. When Gideon realized that it was the angel of the LORD, he exclaimed, "Ah, Sovereign LORD! I have seen the angel of the LORD face to face!" But the LORD said to him, "Peace! <u>Do not be afraid</u>. You are not going to die."

Context: God called Gideon to lead the people against the Midianites. Gideon asked for a sign that the LORD was really calling him, so he prepared a meal offering and put it on a rock. God consumed the food with fire. Gideon was afraid as he thought he was going to die for seeing the Sovereign LORD face to face. Judges 6:1-24

Lessons and Truths:

1.   The LORD can bring peace to me no matter what the circumstances.

2. God will replace my fear with His peace.
3. God encouraged Gideon that the battle would not bring him death. Likewise, my battles will not bring about spiritual death if I know Jesus as my savior.
4. God offers peace, assurance, contentment and safety vs. the world's offering of fear, discouragement, peril and mistrust.

Prayer: Lord, I want to trust You for my safety and receive Your peace. Give me the faith I need to take hold of Your peace and exercise it in my life. You are Sovereign and only You know my future. Help me to rest in Your peace for now and in the future. Amen.

Well-Placed Fear: Psalm 46:1-3

God is our refuge and strength, an ever-present help in trouble. Therefore we will not fear, though the earth give way and the mountains fall into the heart of the sea, though its waters roar and foam and the mountains quake with their surging.

How can I use these truths today?

Where do I need to **appropriate** God's peace _____

Contentment _____

Assurance _____

Safety _____ in my life today?

Where do I need God's encouragement today? _____

_____

_____

Day 21–1 Samuel 12:20–22

Sin of Willfulness

"*Do not be afraid*," Samuel replied. "*You have done all this evil; yet do not turn away from the LORD, but serve the LORD with all your heart. Do not turn away after useless idols. They can do you no good, nor can they rescue you, because they are useless. For the sake of his great name the LORD will not reject his people , because the LORD was pleased to make you his own.*"

Context: The people had sinned against God by asking for a king. Samuel had called upon God to send thunder and rain, and it had awed the people into realizing their sin against God. 1 Samuel 12: 12-25

Lessons and Truths:

1. I am to confess my sins and turn to God.
2. God desires that I serve Him with all my heart.
3. When God tells me no, I need to obey and not willfully demand my own way.
4. Pursuit of idols is futile (useless) and leads to hopelessness.

5.   The LORD is immutable (unchanging) and so is His love for me.

Prayer: Lord, I am often willful and try to demand my own way. I confess that I have tried to run my life my way and need to release it to You in obedience. Give me a heart to please You in my service. Give me joy in my heart and praise on my lips as I serve You each day. Amen.

Well-Placed Fear: 1 Samuel 12:24

But be sure to fear the LORD and serve him faithfully with all your heart; consider what great things he has done for you.

How can I use these truths today?

I confess I have been willful and demanded my own way in

_____

_____

I will be obedient and NOT demand my will but Your will be done in_____

_____

I will praise You for _____

_____

I will claim Your joy in _____

_____ today.

Day 22–1 Kings 17: 13–16

Miraculous Provision

Elijah said to her, "<u>Don't be afraid</u>. Go home and do as you have said. But first make a small cake of bread for me from what you have and bring it to me, and then make something for yourself and your son. For this is what the LORD, the God of Israel, says: 'The jar of flour will not be used up and the jug of oil will not run dry until the day the LORD gives rain on the land.'" She went away and did as Elijah had told her. So there was food everyday for Elijah and for the woman and her family. For the jar of flour was not used up and the jug of oil did not run dry, in keeping with the word of the LORD spoken by Elijah.

Context: There was a drought in the land and the LORD told Elijah to go seek out the widow at Zarephath to give him food. She was preparing to make her final meal and die when Elijah arrived and asked for food. 1 Kings 17:7-16

Lessons and Truths:
1. God knows the future and has a plan for my life.
2. God wants me trusting Him for my survival and provision.

3. Desperate times call for extreme trust in God's sovereignty, not fear!
4. God provided enough for each day. He will do the same for me.
5. Trusting in God's plan is one day at a time.
6. Living a life of trust will bring victory to my life .

Prayer: Lord, help me to have a trusting faith, a faith that does not waver in difficult times but grows stronger in close communion with You. Hear my hearts desires and align them with Your plan for my life to live in victory through You. Amen.

Well-Placed Fear: Psalm 66 :16

Come and listen, all you who fear God; let me tell you what he has done for me.

How I can use these truths today?

List things you know that God has provided for you: _____

_____

_____

Praise Him!

Who can you tell of your experiences with God's provision?

_____

_____

How will telling them strengthen your faith? _____

_____

_____

Day 23-2 Kings 6:15-17

God's Unseen Forces

When the servant of the man of God got up and went out early the next morning, an army with horses and chariots had surrounded the city. "Oh, my lord, what shall we do?" the servant asked. "<u>Don't be afraid,</u>" the prophet answered. "<u>Those who are with us are more than those who are with them.</u>" And Elisha prayed, "O LORD open his eyes so he may see." Then the LORD opened the servant's eyes, and he looked and saw the hills full of horses and chariots of fire all around Elisha.

Context: Elisha had been giving the king of Israel information about the king of Aram's attack plans. Elisha's information came from the Lord. Aram's king got angry and sent his army at night to surround the city where Elisha was so they could capture him. 2 Kings 6:8-17

Lessons and Truths:
1. Just because I don't see God's forces doesn't mean they are not present.
2. I can pray for God's protection as God has unseen

protectors to guard me at all times. God is omnipresent.

3. I can pray for the ability to see and/or recognize those sent by God to help me.

4. God's protection is always big enough to protect me and always bigger than my enemy.

5. God's protection is supernatural and impenetrable, chariots of fire!

Prayer: Oh God, may I trust in Your provision and protection which far surpasses anything I can even imagine. Help me to recognize Your protection and thank you for it. Thank you that You are omnipresent and ever vigilant for Your servants. Help me to trust You fully in times of need so that You can have the glory and praise! Amen.

Well-Placed Fear: Psalm 33:8-11

Let all the earth <u>fear the LORD</u>; let all the people of the world <u>revere him</u>. For he spoke, and it came to be; he commanded, and it stood firm. The LORD foils the plans of the nations; he thwarts the purposes of the peoples. But the plans of the LORD stand firm forever, the purposes of his heart through all generations.

How can I use these truths today?

Where do I (or someone I know) need protection in my (their) life? _____

_____

Pray, asking God to meet this need and show you the help he has/is sending. Praise Him!

Completion God's Way

avid also said to Solomon his son, "Be strong and courageous, and do the work. <u>Do not be afraid or discouraged,</u> for the LORD God, my God, is with you. He will not fail you or forsake you until the work for the service of the temple of the LORD is finished."

Context: David called all the people of Israel together and told them of God's specific plans for building the temple. God had chosen Solomon, David's son, to build the temple and this verse gives David's commission to Solomon. 1Chronicles 28:1-21

<u>Lessons and Truths:</u>
1. The Lord gives me courage and strength.
2. The Lord gives me enough of whatever I need to finish His work. I need only remain faithful to it.
3. God wants His work completed.
4. God will never fail me nor forsake me.
5. Nothing/No one can take God's presence away from me as He promises to be with me always.

Prayer: Lord, give me the courage and strength I need to accomplish Your work. Give me the will and faith to trust in You always. Help me to remain faithful to the work You have given me to do, the people You have me serving, and helping in Your name. Thank you for the promise You have given to be with me always. Amen.

Well-Placed Fear: Psalm 64:9-10

All mankind will fear; they will proclaim the works of God and ponder what he has done. Let the righteous rejoice in the LORD and take refuge in him; let all the upright in heart praise him!

How can I use these truths today?

What work has God given me to do? _____

_____

Am I being faithful to this work? Yes, thank and praise Him! No, what do you need to recommit to Him?_____

_____

Do you see a place where Satan is trying to take away your joy in serving or your confidence in seeing the job to completion?

_____

_____

_____

Commit this to prayer right now!

Watch God Deliver

He said: "Listen , King Jehoshaphat and all who live in Judah and Jerusalem! This is what the LORD says to you: '*Do not be afraid or discouraged because of this vast army. For the battle is not yours, but God's. Tomorrow march down against them. They will be climbing up by the Pass of Ziz, and you will find them at the end of the gorge in the Desert of Jeruel. You will not have to fight this battle. Take up your positions; stand firm and see the deliverance the LORD will give you. O Judah and Jerusalem. Do not be afraid; do not be discouraged. Go out to face them tomorrow, and the LORD will be with you.*'"

Context: The Moabites and Ammonites came to make war against King Jehoshaphat with a vast army. Jehoshaphat sought help from God, and God asked him to trust Him for the victory. 2 Chronicles 20:1-29

Lessons and Truths:
1.   God will fight my battles if I trust Him and am obedient.
2.   Trusting God involves following His way for victory.

3.   My job in the battle: Be in the position He has for me
                          Stand firm
                          Watch for His deliverance
                          Praise Him!
4.   God will do all the work.
5.   He promises to be with me, and I am not to allow discouragement or fear to creep into my life.

Prayer: Oh Lord, I know the battles I face are Yours and that You have victory for me. Help me to be where You want me to be, to stand firm in Your Word and wait and watch for Your deliverance. Give me strength to trust You fully and not give into despair or discouragement. Amen.

Well-Placed Fear: 2 Chronicles 20:29-30

The fear of God came upon all the kingdom of the countries when they heard how the LORD had fought against the enemies of Israel. And the kingdom of Jehoshaphat was at peace, for his God has given him rest on every side.

How can I use these truths today?

We learn from past victories. Where have you experienced victory over a battle, and then had God's peace on every side?

_____

_____

What battle are you facing today where you need to? Be in position, stand firm and watch for His deliverance. _____

_____

_____

Enemies Defeated

He appointed military officers over the people and assembled them before him in the square at the city gate and encouraged them with these words: "Be strong and courageous. Do not be afraid or discouraged because of the king of Assyria and the vast army with him, for there is a greater power with us than with him. With him is only the arm of flesh, but with us is the LORD our God to help us and to fight our battles." And the people gained confidence from what Hezekiah the king of Judah said.

Context: Sennacherib, the king of Assyria, had come to invade Judah. He had laid siege to the cities. King Hezekiah saw him approaching Jerusalem and gathered his people to fight against him. God intervened and totally annihilated Sennacherib. 2 Chronicles 32:1-23

Lessons and Truths:
1. God's power, with me, is greater than any enemy.
2. My confidence is in God, therefore NO FEAR!

3. My adversary only has help from this world; I have God to fight for and with me.
4. God's Word gives confidence.
5. The apostle John reconfirmed this in 1 John 4:4.

    You, dear children, are from God and have overcome them because the one who is in you is greater than the one who is in the world.

Prayer: Lord, I praise You that You are greater than any enemy I will ever face. I can have confidence in Your Word and take comfort and strength in Your presence. Help me to live today in faith believing You for victory. Amen.

Well-Placed Fear: Luke 1:68, 74-75

"Praise be to the Lord, the God of Israel, because he has come and has redeemed his people…. to rescue us from the hand of our enemies and to enable us to serve him without fear in holiness and righteousness before him all our days."

How can I use these truths today?

Where am I **falsely thinking** that my problem is bigger than God can handle? _____

_____

_____

Claim the promise in Luke 1: 37 over this problem. *"For nothing is impossible with God."*

Remember Hebrews 11: 6. *"And without faith it is impossible to please God, because anyone who comes to him must believe that he exists and that he rewards those who earnestly seek him."*

Day 27–Nehemiah 4:13–15

God Frustrates Enemies

*T*herefore I stationed some of the people behind the lowest points of the wall at the exposed places, posting them by families, with their swords, spears and bows. After I looked things over, I stood up and said to the nobles, the officials and the rest of the people, "*Don't be afraid of them*. Remember the Lord, who is great and awesome, and fight for your brothers, your sons and your daughters, your wives and your homes." When our enemies heard that we were aware of their plot and that God had frustrated it, we all returned to the wall, each to his own work.

Context: Nehemiah had returned to Jerusalem from Babylon with a group of Israelites. They were working to restore Jerusalem and needed to rebuild the wall surrounding the city. There were many in the area who opposed the rebuilding and sought to defeat their efforts. Nehemiah 4:7-23

Lessons and Truths:

1.   Doing work for the Lord requires organization,

determination and faith that God will help you to see it to completion.

2. God knows the enemy's plans.

3. No plan devised by the enemy is greater than God.

4. After the crisis has passed, God requires that I continue with diligence and watchfulness to guard against Satan's future attacks.

Prayer: Lord, help me to be serious in doing Your work. Give me the organization skills I need, determination to see the work completed, and faith in You to finish the good work You have started in me. You know the beginning from the end and I would ask Your protection against attacks by Satan. Thwart his attempts to slow or interrupt Your work and give me diligence to persevere. Amen.

Well-Placed Fear: 2 Chronicles 19:9

He(Jehoshaphat) gave them these orders: "You must serve faithfully and wholeheartedly in the fear of the LORD."

How can I use these truths today?

Where do I feel I am most lacking? Organization, determination or faith? _____

_____

Pray now for God to fill this need in a mighty way.

Where does God want me to be watchful for Satan's attack?

_____

_____

Day 28-Isaiah 7:3- 4

God's Crisis Admonitions

*T*hen *the Lord said to Isaiah, "Go out, you and your son Shear-Jashub, to meet Ahaz at the end of the aqueduct of the Upper Pool, on the road to the Washerman's Field. Say to him, 'Be careful, keep calm and don't be afraid. Do not lose heart because of these two smoldering stubs of firewood-because of the fierce anger of Rezin and Aram and the son of Remaliah."*

Context: Isaiah was the prophet during Ahaz's reign in Judah. The enemy kings referred to as smoldering stubs, Rezin and Aram, had allied together to come against Israel. The Lord spoke to Isaiah and sent this encouraging message to Ahaz. Isaiah 7:1-9

Lessons and Truths:

1.   God is sovereign and knows what <u>will happen</u> and what <u>will not happen</u>

2.   In the face of crisis God desires me to be:
              - careful-not reckless in actions, or impatient
              - calm-not fretful, worried or overcome with fear, no

panic allowed

- committed to Him-do not lose heart, stand firm in faith

3.   No matter what the circumstances look like, He is greater than anything I can possibly face.

Prayer: Father, You know what lies ahead for me this day and in the future. Take me and give me a spirit of calm, patience in action and commitment to You. Erase from me all worry and doubt as You are indeed sovereign and greater and more capable than any adversary I will ever face. Help me to live today victoriously in You. Amen.

Well-Placed Fear: Ecclesiastes 3:14

I know that everything God does will endure forever; nothing can be added to it and nothing taken from it. God does it so that men will (fear) revere him.

How can I use these truths today?

In the problems I am facing today:

Where do I need caution? _____

Where (when) do I need to be calm? _____

Where am I in danger of losing heart and need to be recommitted to Him and stand firm? _____

How can I turn today's challenges into an opportunity to trust and praise Him? _____

Day 29-Isaiah 8:11-14a

God is Enough!

The LORD spoke to me with his strong hand upon me, warning me not to follow the way of this people. He said: "Do not call conspiracy everything that these people call conspiracy; <u>do not fear what they fear, and do not dread it</u>. The LORD Almighty is the one you are to regard as holy, he is the one you are to fear, he is the one you are to dread, and he will be a sanctuary; but for both houses of Israel he will be a stone that causes men to stumble and a rock that makes them fall."

Context: God is speaking to King Ahaz of Israel through the prophet Isaiah. He does not want Ahaz to make alliances with others against Assyria. God wants Ahaz to depend upon Him, as God alone is to be Israel's defense. Isaiah 8:11-17

Lessons and Truths:

1. God want me to rely on Him alone. No alliances or compromises are need to defeat my enemies. God alone is sufficient.

2. Knowing God, I do not need to fear the world and circumstances like non-believers do.
3. God is holy.
4. My reverence (fear) should be reserved for God alone.
5. God will literally trip up my enemies and defeat them.
6. God is my refuge.

Prayer: Lord, help me to trust that all I need is You to be victorious against my enemies. You are holy and worthy of my devotion and trust. You are my refuge and have a plan to thwart my enemies. Increase my faith so that I can rely solely on You day by day. Amen.

Well-Placed Fear: Isaiah 8:13

The LORD Almighty is the one you are to regard as holy, he is the one you are to fear, he is the one you are to dread.

How can I use these truths today?

What is making me feel that I need to compromise my faith to succeed? _____

_____

_____

Where am I harboring fear as if I am an unbeliever? _____

_____

_____

Ask God to stand with you in faith and take away your fear.

Day 30–Isaiah 37:5-7

Hearsay, Give it to God

*W*hen *King Hezekiah's officials came to Isaiah, Isaiah said to them, "Tell your master, 'This is what the LORD says:* <u>*Do not be afraid of what you have heard*</u>*- those words which the underlings of the king of Assyria have blasphemed to me. Listen! I am going to put a spirit in him so that when he hears a certain report, he will return to his own country, and there I will have him cut down with the word.'"*

Context: King Hezekiah was worried as the king of Assyria (Sennacherib) had sent messengers to Jerusalem to belittle God and say that Hezekiah was wrong to put trust in God to save them from the coming attack. Isaiah 37:1-20

Lessons and Truths:

1. When I hear disparaging news, I need to give it to God as He does not want me to be fearful. He wants me confident in His ability to overcome all obstacles.

2. God has a plan for victory. Here, He shared it with King Hezekiah to help relieve his distress. God's Word

will soothe, comfort and assure me of God's might and sovereignty.

3. God will fight my enemies and assures me that they will be dealt with as He deems appropriate.

4. Faith in God's ability, might, sovereignty and power will overcome fear.

Prayer: Lord, help me to feel Your comfort and believe in Your sovereign power when I face adversity. Keep my fears away and do not let me be led astray by the things I see and hear. Cause me to focus on your ability to overcome and give victory. Increase my faith as I strive to please You. Amen.

Well-Placed Fear: Psalm 103:11-13

For as high as the heavens are above the earth, so great is his love for those who fear him; as far as the east is from the west, so far has he removed our transgressions from us. As a father has compassion on his children, so the LORD has compassion on those who fear him.

How can I use these truths today?

How does knowing God loves, forgives and has compassion upon you transform your thoughts about his ability to give you victory in your present fearful circumstance? _____

_____

What have you heard lately that has caused you to be fearful?

_____

Do as the LORD commands. Do not be afraid and give your fears to Him!!!

Day 31–Isaiah 41:9–10

We're Upheld by Jesus

I took you from the ends of the earth, from its farthest corners I called you. I said, 'You are my servant'; I have chosen you and have not rejected you. So do not fear, for I am with you, do not be dismayed, for I am your God. I will strengthen you and help you; I will uphold you with my righteous right hand.

Context: These words from God were written by Isaiah to cause the Israelites to remember that God had called them, and that He would be with them. They were facing future captivity due to their own sinful ways and Isaiah's words were to be an encouragement to them in the present as well as in the future. Isaiah 41:1-10

Lessons and Truths:
1. God is sovereign and I was chosen by God to serve Him.
2. His presence dispels fear.
3. Knowing He is my God frees me from discouragement as Romans 8: 31 reminds me. *If God is for us who can be*

against us? Nothing/No one can withstand the power of God.

4. God promises to provide strength and help.
5. God promises to uphold me through Jesus, who is His righteous right hand.

Prayer: Lord, help me to lean on Your presence to dispel my fears and trust in You for my future. Help me to believe in my very core that You are sovereign and greater than all. Lord, I want to trust that Your strength and help will be totally sufficient for all my needs. Thank you for Jesus and His upholding hand that has me firmly in His grasp. Help me to live victoriously, depending upon You and Your strength each day. Amen.

Well-Placed Fear: Romans 8:15-16

For you did not receive a spirit that make you a slave again to fear, but you received the Spirit of sonship. And by him we cry, "Abba, Father." The Spirit himself testifies with our spirit that we are God's children.

How can I use these truths today?

How does knowing that I am God's child help to dispel my fear for the things I am facing today? _____

_____

_____

God promises His strength and help. Ask Him for it. Where do you need strength and help – be specific. _____

_____

_____

Day 32–Isaiah 41:13–14

Hand Holding with God

"*For I am the LORD, your God, who takes hold of your right hand and says to you, <u>Do not fear</u>; I will help you. <u>Do not be afraid</u>, O worm Jacob, O little Israel, for I myself will help you," declares the LORD, your Redeemer, the Holy One of Israel.*

Context: Isaiah is giving words from God to encourage the Israelites now and in the future. The nation was straying from God and would reap the consequences of those actions by captivity for 70 years in Babylon. The term, worm of Jacob, refers to their lowly state when in captivity. Isaiah 41:11-20

Lessons and Truths:
1. God promises to personally lead, guide, comfort and help me.
2. By holding my hand, God shows He cares for me.
3. God promises to help me. He knows my circumstances and how to resolve my problems.
4. Since God will attend to me personally, I mean something

to Him and have value in His eyes. I am loved by the God of the universe.

5. He reminds me that He is Holy, His character is pure and blameless, and He is my redeemer.

Prayer: Lord, thank you for personally caring for me and touching me. Thank you for being accessible to my cries for help and for Your promised deliverance. You can deliver me from those circumstances that are causing me to be fearful. I know that I am loved by You and that You value me. Help me to trust in Your care and honor You with my faith and service. Amen.

Well-Placed Fear: Psalm 147:10-11

His pleasure is not in the strength of the horse, nor his delight in the legs of a man; the LORD delights in those who <u>fear him</u>, who put their hope in his unfailing love.

How can I use these truths today?

Where do I need God's personal touch? _____

_____

_____

God wants to delight in me. I need to place my trust and reverence in Him, and He promises hope in His unfailing love. What do I need to trust Him with today so that He can delight in me?

_____

_____

_____

Day 33-Isaiah 43:1- 5

God is Personal

But now, this is what the LORD says- he who created you, O Jacob, he who formed you, O Israel; "Fear not, for I have redeemed you; I have summoned you by name; you are mine. When you pass through the waters, I will be with you; and when you pass through the rivers, they will not sweep over you. When you walk through the fire, you will not be burned; the flames will not set you ablaze. For I am the LORD, your God, the Holy One of Israel, your Savior; I give Egypt for your ransom, Cush and Seba in your stead. Since you are precious and honored in my sight, and because I love you, I will give men in exchange for you, and people in exchange for your life. Do not be afraid, for I am with you; I will bring your children from the east and gather you from the west."

Context: Isaiah is giving words of encouragement to the people of Israel. God is reassuring them that they will be brought back from their exile in Babylon. He reminds them of how He brought them out of Egypt and is sovereign in dealing with nations. Isaiah 43:1-13

Lessons and Truths:

1. God is the creator of everything and sovereign over all.
2. God has redeemed me; He did all the work.
3. He knows me by name and I belong to Him!
4. No matter what the circumstances, even cataclysmic events, He is in control.
5. I am precious in His sight and honored by Him.
6. He loves me.
7. He plans to see me though and bring me to himself, no matter how it looks to me right now.
8. He promises to be with me always.

Prayer: Lord, I can scarcely grasp the idea that You know me by name and that I am precious in your sight. Your promise to be with me always brings me great comfort. I am so undeserving and unable to do any of the work of being redeemed, You did it all. Thank you! Help me to live today like a loved one of the Most Holy One as a child of God who is loved and cared for in all circumstances. Amen.

Well-Placed Fear: Psalm 96:4-5

For great is the LORD and most worthy of praise; he is to be feared above all gods. For all the gods of the nations are idols, but the LORD made the heavens.

How can I use these truths today?

What am I facing today where I need to be assured of God's presence and love? _____

_____

Day 34-Isaiah 44:2-3

God Cares for Me

This is what the LORD says- he who made you, who formed you in the womb, and who will help you: <u>*Do not be afraid*</u>*, O Jacob, my servant, Jeshurun, who I have chosen. For I will pour water on the thirsty land, and streams on the dry ground; I will pour out my Spirit on your offspring, and my blessing on your descendants.*

Context: Isaiah continues to give encouragement to the Israelites to sustain them during the coming 70 years of captivity in Babylon. He is promising restoration to their land and blessings to come. Jeshurun refers to the nation Israel. Isaiah 44:1-5

Lessons and Truths:

1. God created and formed me in the womb; He knew me even before I was born.
2. I am chosen by God and special to him.
3. God promises to help me during my life.
4. The Creator of the universe is personally invested in my life and promises to help me. How much better can it get?

5.   He promises to pour out His Spirit upon me and bless me.
6.   As a child of God, my descendants and I will receive blessings.
7.   God says I can live without fear because He chose me, blesses me and helps me.

Prayer: Lord, I am so unworthy of Your special treatment. Help me to live each day knowing that I am loved by You, cared for and able to be filled with Your Holy Spirit. Thank you for choosing me to be Yours. Help me to live like I believe that I am loved by You. Amen.

Well-Placed Fear: Psalm 103:17-18

But from everlasting to everlasting the LORD's love is with those who <u>fear him</u>, and his righteousness with their children's children- with those who keep his covenant and remember to obey his precepts.

How can I use these truths today?

Where am I experiencing fear in my life right now? _____

_____

_____

Where do I need a special blessing? _____

_____

_____

Pray right now for victory over this fear and for a special blessing.

God, Like No Other

"*This is what the LORD says- Israel's King and Redeemer, the LORD Almighty: I am the first and I am the last; apart from me there is no God. Who then is like me? Let him proclaim it. Let him declare and lay out before me what has happened since I established my ancient people, and what is yet to come- yes, let him foretell what will come. <u>Do not tremble, do not be afraid</u>. Did I not proclaim this and foretell it long ago? You are my witnesses. Is there any God besides me? No, there is no other Rock; I know not one.*"

Context: The nation Israel has strayed into idolatry. God is reminding them though the prophet Isaiah that He is God, the One and Only. Isaiah 44:6-11

Lessons and Truths:

1. God alone is God. There is no other and He is sovereign.
2. God was there at the beginning and will be there at the end.
3. He is omniscient. He knows all: past, present and future.

4. Israel's history showed God's power to foretell future events.
5. God is a rock – solid, stable, the foundation of my life.
6. God is unique. There is no other like Him,

Prayer: Lord, I know that fear comes from not trusting in You. Help me to better understand Your awesome character that is steadfast, all knowing and greater than any force in the entire universe. Thank you, Lord, for being the same yesterday, today and forever. With You, there is no room for fear as You are indeed sovereign. Amen.

Well-Placed Fear: Psalm 85:8-9

I will listen to what God the LORD will say; he promises peace to his people, his saints- but let them not return to folly. Surely his salvation is near those who fear him, that his glory may dwell in our land.

How can I use these truths today?

God is omniscient – all knowing, steadfast – always dependable, and omnipotent – all powerful.

What do these characteristics of God mean to me? _____

_____

_____

Knowing these things about God's character, what do I need to surrender to Him and His power? _____

_____

_____

Day 36-Isaiah 51:7-8

God's Word Protects

" *Hear me, you who know what is right, you people who have my law in your hearts:* <u>*Do not fear the reproach of men or be terrified by their insults*</u>. *For the moth will eat them up like a garment; the worm will devour them like wool. But my righteousness will last forever, my salvation through all generations.*"

Context: Isaiah continues to deliver God's message to His people who believe in Him. He gives them solid encouragement in the face of adversity. Isaiah 51:1-8

Lessons and Truths:

1.   Knowing God and having His words in my heart protects me.

2.   Others seek to put me down, scorn, terrorize, and hurt me, but God promises to deal with them, devouring them.

3.   The image is that He will put holes in them, either literally or figuratively, so that they will be destroyed.

4.   God promises His righteousness and salvation are eternal.

Prayer: Lord, help me to cling to Your Word and do what is right in Your eyes. I know Your righteousness is eternal and You are the one who has saved me. Let me leave the worries caused by others – their hurts, scorn and demoralizing thoughts at Your feet. Take care of them as You have promised. Lift me up and bring me out victorious. Amen.

Well-Placed Fear: Psalm 119:105, 120

The word is a lamp to my feet and a light for my path........
My flesh trembles in <u>fear of you</u>; I stand in awe of your laws.

How can I use these truths today?

What fears do I perceive that come from others? _____

_____

_____

I know I can trust Your Word to light my way and that fear should be directed at You. I want to name each of these fears and give them to You. _____

_____

_____

Please deal with them as You have promised and give me an extra portion of faith to confront these fears as I live today and leave them with You. Amen.

Day 37-Isaiah 54:4-5

Holy Redeemer

"*Do not be afraid; you will not suffer shame. Do not fear disgrace; you will not be humiliated. You will forget the shame of your youth and remember no more the reproach of your widowhood. For your Maker is your husband- the LORD Almighty is his name- the Holy One of Israel is your Redeemer; he is called the God of all the earth.*"

Context: The Lord knew that the Israelites would look back on their history with shame and disgrace over their slavery in Egypt and captivity in Babylon. He encourages them through Isaiah to trust in His character. Isaiah 54: 1-17

Lessons and Truths:

1. The Lord Jesus can cover my shame and alleviate the pain it causes.
2. He can cause me to forget things from my mind so that I will no longer dwell on them.
3. God lists for me the roles He desires to exercise in my life if I will turn to Him and trust Him: Maker (Creator),

Husband (loving caretaker, companion), Almighty God (all-powerful God), Holy One (pure, spotless), Redeemer (Savior), sovereign God of all.

Prayer: God, I want You in my life as sovereign LORD. Fill up my life so that former disgrace and shame are erased from my memory, and I am consumed by Your love. Heal my broken spirit and redeem me for Your work. Amen

Well-Placed Fear: Micah 7:17b-19

They (nations) will come trembling out of their dens; they will turn in <u>fear</u> to the LORD our God and <u>will be afraid of you</u>. Who is a God like you, who pardons sin and forgives the transgression of the remnant of his inheritance? You do not stay angry forever but delight to show mercy. ***You will again have compassion on us; you will tread our sins underfoot and hurl all our iniquities into the depths of the sea.***

How can I use these truths today?

What do I need God to graciously erase from my memory that is causing me fear, anxiety or worry?_____

_____

What sins do I need to confess and repent of so that God can remove them far away from me, never to return?_____

_____

What role do I need God to exercise in my life today? _____

_____

_____

Chosen with a Purpose

The word of the LORD came to me, saying, "Before I formed you in the womb I knew you, before you were born I set you apart; I appointed you as a prophet to the nations." "Ah, Sovereign LORD," I said, "I do not know how to speak; I am only a child." But the LORD said to me, "Do not say, 'I am only a child.' You must go to everyone I send you to and say whatever I command you. <u>Do not be afraid of them</u>, for I am with you and will rescue you," declares the LORD.

Context: God called Jeremiah to be His prophet to the nation of Israel starting in the reign of Josiah until they went into exile in Babylon. He was their prophet for 47 years. This is his call from God to serve Him. Twice in this commissioning passage (verses 8, 17) God tells Jeremiah to not be afraid. Jeremiah 1:1-19

<u>Lessons and Truths:</u>

1.   God knew me before I was born and chose me to be His own.

2. God has a purpose and work for my life, just as he had for Jeremiah.
3. God can and will use me to do His work – no excuses allowed.
4. Following God's way requires obedience.
5. To counteract my fear, God promises His presence with me and assures me of rescue.

Prayer: Lord, You know me personally and have a specific work You want me to do. Show me Your way. Give me the courage, determination and focus to see Your work to completion. Thank you for the assurance of Your presence with me each day and knowledge that You know all that is to happen and have my rescue already planned. Amen.

Well-Placed Fear: Psalm 139:13-14

For you created my inmost being; you knit me together in my mother's womb. I praise you because I am fearfully and wonderfully made; your works are wonderful, I know that full well.

How can I use these truths today?

What excuses am I presenting to God, saying I can't possibly work for Him?_____

_____

How will I follow God in obedience today?_____

_____

_____

Day 39-Jeremiah 10:4-6,10

Powerless Idols

They adorn it with silver and gold; they fasten it with hammer and nails so it will not totter. Like a scarecrow in a melon patch, their idols cannot speak; they must be carried because they cannot walk. Do not fear them; they can do no harm nor can they do any good. No one is like you, O LORD; you are great, and your name is might in power. ... But the LORD is the true God; he is the living God, the eternal King. When he is angry, the earth trembles; the nations cannot endure his wrath.

Context: Jeremiah is giving God's message to the people of Judah that idols are worthless and without any power. God reminds them that He alone is living and powerful. Jeremiah 10:1-10

Lessons and Truths:

1. Idols are man-made, mute, harmless and have no power over me unless I allow it. Today's idols might be money, advancement, materialism and power over others.

2. It can be anything that takes the place of God being #1 in my life.
3. God has power and might.
4. God is living and eternal.
5. God has power over His creation and I can feel the effects of his powerful presence.

Prayer: Lord, show me the things that I have placed in front of You in my life. Help me to put them in proper priority or even eliminate them from my life altogether. Fill me with Your living spirit that I might live each day for You. Amen.

Well-Placed Fear: Proverbs 15:14-16

The discerning heart seeks knowledge, but the mouth of a fool feeds on folly. All the days of the oppressed are wretched, but the cheerful heart has a continual feast. <u>Better a little with the fear of the LORD</u> than great wealth with turmoil.

How can I use these truths today?

What idols am I placing before God? _____

_____

_____

With God as #1, what are my other priorities? _____

_____

_____

Pray for His strength to eliminate idols and keep Godly priorities.

Hard Places with God

" '*So do not fear, O Jacob my servant; do not be dismayed, O Israel', declares the LORD. 'I will surely save you out of a distant place, your descendants from the land of their exile. Jacob will again have peace and security and no one will make him afraid. I am with you and will save you,' declares the LORD. 'Though I completely destroy all the nations among which I scatter you, I will not completely destroy you. I will discipline you but only with justice; I will not let you go entirely unpunished.'*"

Context: Jeremiah was God's messenger for 50 years to the people of Israel. Here, he delivers words of encouragement and hope for their coming exile. Jeremiah 30:1-21

Lessons and Truths:
1. God knows my hard (distant) places and promises to restore me.
2. God promises peace and security in Him.
3. God can and will save!

4. God disciplines me with justice. Thank goodness for His mercy!

5. My sinful actions result in consequences.

Prayer: Lord, You are indeed merciful and keep Your promises. You know where I am struggling today, reach down and touch me where I am. Show me where I am sinning that I may repent and seek Your mercy. Amen.

Well-Placed Fear: Psalm 118:4-6

Let those who fear the LORD say: "*His love endures forever.*" *In my anguish I cried to the LORD, and he answered by setting me free. The LORD is with me; I will not be afraid. What can man do to me?*

How can I use these truths today?

How have I experienced God's love in my life? _____

_____

_____

What hard place am I in that I need God's touch and mercy?

_____

_____

_____

Day 41-Jeremiah 42:11-16

Deliverance from Fear

Do not be afraid of the king of Babylon, whom you now fear. Do not be afraid of him, declares the LORD, for I am with you and will save you and deliver you from his hands. I will show you compassion so that he will have compassion on you and restore you to your land. "However, if you say, 'We will not stay in this land,' and so disobey the LORD your God, and if you say, 'No, we will go and live in Egypt, where we will not see war or hear the trumpet or be hungry for bread,' then hear the word of the LORD, O remnant of Judah. This is what the LORD Almighty, the God of Israel, say: 'If you are determined to go to Egypt and you do go to settle there, then the sword you fear will overtake you there, and the famine you dread will follow you into Egypt, and there you will die.

Context: Jeremiah interceded with God on behalf of the rebel leader Johanan. He feared the king of Babylon's reprisals as the rebel leader Ishmael had killed the king's governor and many others. The tiny remnant of Jews needed the Lord's help. God told them to stay in Judah and not flee to Egypt, or they would suffer consequences. Jeremiah 41:16 - 43:13

Lessons and Truths:

1. God knows the reasons for my fears.
2. God treats me with compassion and grace.
3. God promises hope, presence, salvation and deliverance in place of fears.
4. God can/does manipulate my enemies into working things in my favor.
5. Following God and receiving His blessings requires obedience.
6. Disobedience always results in consequences.

Prayer: Lord, You know my fears even better than I do myself. Help me to see Your compassion and grace today. Bring your hope, presence, salvation and deliverance into my life. Take care of my enemies and remove them from my thoughts. Help me to be obedient to You. Amen

Well-Placed Fear: Proverbs 14:16 and 26

A wise man fears the LORD and shuns evil, but a fool is hotheaded and reckless.

....He who fears the LORD has a secure fortress, and for his children it will be a refuge.

How can I use these truths today?

What disobedient action or attitude do I need to confess right now? _____

Where do I need *hope, God's presence, his salvation or deliverance* in my life? _____

_____

Peace and Security

"*Do not fear, O Jacob my servant; do not be dismayed, O Israel. I will surely save you out of a distance place, your descendants from the land of their exile. Jacob will again have peace and security, and no one will make him afraid. Do not fear, O Jacob my servant, for I am with you," declares the LORD. "Though I completely destroy all the nations among which I scatter you, I will not completely destroy you. I will discipline you but only with justice; I will not let you go entirely unpunished."*

Context: Jeremiah was prophet of Israel during the last kings prior to their exportation and captivity in Babylon. The people were sinning and straying away from God. Jeremiah has words to encourage and yet to hold them accountable for their sins. Jeremiah 46: 27-28

Lessons and Truths:
1. God can save me out of the places where I find myself.
2. God promises peace and security in His care.

3. God controls the nations surrounding me.
4. My actions/sins will not go unpunished; God will discipline me.
5. God's discipline will not destroy me but will show justice and mercy.
6. God will not deal mercifully with my enemies.

Prayer: Lord, help me to not lose heart in the place where I find myself today. Help me to claim Your salvation, peace and security for my own. Help me to put away my fears. Lord, forgive me for my actions that dishonor You, my thoughts that stray from You and my will that is not obedient. I would turn to You today and cling to the hope that You promise. Amen.

Well-Placed Fear: 2 Corinthians 7:1

Since we have these promises, dear friends, let us purify ourselves from every-thing that contaminates body and spirit, perfecting holiness out of reverence (fear) for God.

How can I use these truths today?

In what circumstances do I find myself that I need God's help?

_____

_____

Did my own sinful nature contribute to me being in this place?

_____

_____

If yes, what do I need to confess and repent? _____

_____

Day 43-Lamentations 3:55-58

God Hears

I called on your name, O LORD, from the depths of the pit. You heard my plea: "Do not close your ears to my cry for relief." You came near when I called you, and you said, "Do not fear." O Lord, you took up my case; you redeemed my life.

Context: Jeremiah wrote these words after the complete destruction of Jerusalem by the Babylonian forces and deportation of the people to Babylon. Jeremiah pleads with God to again come to his defense and that of the nation Israel as He has done in the past. Lamentations 3:55-66.

Lessons and Truths:

1. God hears my prayers no matter where I am.
2. God does not have human ears; he will always hear me.
3. He responds to my call and brings relief of spirit.
4. God's presence dispels fear.
5. God is my redeemer and advocate. He is in my corner!

Prayer: Lord, I am so thankful that You hear my prayers. There is no place I can be that You will not hear me. Help me to not despair and call upon You in times of need. You promise to always be with me, and I trust Your presence will keep my fears away. Amen.

Well-Placed Fear: Psalm 34:11, 15

Come, my children, listen to me; I will teach you the <u>fear</u> of the LORD......The eyes of the LORD are on the righteous and his ears are attentive to their cry;

How can I use these truths today?

For what do I need to cry out to the Lord? _____

_____

_____

Where do I need God to be my advocate? _____

_____

_____

Thank you, LORD, for hearing my cry and giving me confidence in You today. Amen.

Day 44-Ezekiel 2:6 and 3:9

Facing Rebellion

" *And* nd you, son of man, <u>do not be afraid of them or their words. Do not be afraid</u>, though briers and thorns are all around you and you live among scorpions. <u>Do not be afraid of what they say or terrified by them</u>, though they are a rebellious house.....I will make your forehead like the hardest stone, harder than flint. <u>Do not be afraid of them or terrified by them</u>, though they are a rebellious house."

Context: God called Ezekiel to speak His words to the people of Israel in Babylon. They were a rebellious people in spirit and actions. God knew that Ezekiel would have difficult and often discouraging times ahead. Ezekiel 2:1-3:15

Lessons and Truths:

1.   God knows about the 'briers and thorns' that surround me in life.

2.   God wants me to recognize their 'words' as that, just words and not instruments that should produce fear.

3. God will prepare me to face my adversaries. I need to stand firm with His protection.
4. He can make me strong in body and mind like nothing else that exists.
5. I need to see my adversaries as rebellious against God not me.

Prayer: Lord, make me aware of Your presence and help me to stand firm in both body and mind, focusing on You. Provide a shield around about me to protect me from my adversaries' hard words, thorny places and stinging actions. Give me Your peace in living and dealing with those who are rebellious towards You. Amen.

Well Placed Fear: Revelation 14:7

He (angel) said in a loud voice, "Fear God and give him glory, because the hour of his judgment has come. Worship him who made the heavens, the earth, the sea and the springs of water."

How can I use these truths today?

What thorny places or hard words am I facing right now?

_____

_____

Where am I facing opposition to God's work that He has given me to do?_____

_____

How can I give God glory today? _____

_____

Day 45–Daniel 10:10–12

Set Your Mind on God

A hand touched me and set me trembling on my hands and knees. He said, "Daniel, you who are highly esteemed, consider carefully the words I am about to speak to you, and stand up, for I have now been sent to you." And when he said this to me, I stood up trembling. Then he continued, "<u>Do not be afraid, Daniel.</u> Since the first day that you set your mind to gain understanding and to humble yourself before your God, your words were heard, and I have come in response to them."

Context: Daniel, serving King Cyrus of Persia while in captivity in Babylon, received a vision/revelation from God. Scholars believe the speaker to be the pre-incarnate Christ. Daniel 10:1-14

Lessons and Truths:

1.   With Christ as my Savior, my prayers go directly to God. He will come to help me when I ask.

2.   When I set my mind and focus on God, I will receive understanding.

3.   God desires humility as I approach Him.

4.   God's Word requires careful attention and consideration.

5.   Daniel was afraid of the heavenly being that appeared to him. As a believer, I have the Holy Spirit living within me and I can call upon God for help at any time. His indwelling presence alleviates my fear.

Prayer: Lord, help me to humble myself by casting off pride, arrogance and self-boasting. Help me to look only to You for understanding and answers to my daily circumstances. Give me a spirit of reliance upon You. Amen.

Well-Placed Fear: Psalm 2:11 and Psalm 25:9

  2:11- Serve the LORD with fear and rejoice with trembling.

  25: 9- He guides the humble in what is right and teaches them his way.

How can I use these truths today?

Where do I need to be humble before God? _____

_____

_____

Where do I need to call upon the LORD today?_____

_____

_____

Thank you, Father, for what You will do in and through me today. Amen.

Strength Provided

Again the one who looked like a man touched me and gave me strength. "Do not be afraid, O man highly esteemed," *he said. "Peace! Be strong now; be strong." When he spoke to me, I was strengthened and said, "Speak, my lord, since you have given me strength."*

Context: Daniel is receiving a prophetic vision about the future. The man giving him the vision is believed, by scholars, to be the pre-incarnate Christ. Daniel 10:15-21

Lessons and Truths:

1. God can touch me; He is concerned about me personally.
2. God's touch brings strength.
3. God knew in advance of Daniel's need for strength. He knows in advance what I need, too.
4. God wants peace and strength for me when I serve Him.
5. God's touch gives courage.

Prayer: Lord, touch me and give me Your strength. You know the things I am facing that are causing me to be fearful. Give me courage as I face today. Amen.

Well-Placed Fear: Psalm 46:1-3 and 10

God is our refuge and strength, an ever-present help in trouble. Therefore <u>we will not fear</u> though the earth give way and the mountains fall into the heart of the sea, though its waters roar and foam and the mountains quake with their surging. Selah…. "Be still, and know that I am God; I will be exalted among the nations, I will be exalted in the earth."

How can I use these truths today?

Where do I need God's strength to eliminate my fears?_____

_____

_____

Lord, give me your peace over the following situations/people.

_____

_____

_____

Amen.

Joy and Contentment

Be not afraid, O land; be glad and rejoice. Surely the LORD has done great things. Be not afraid, O wild animals, for the open pastures are becoming green. The trees are bearing their fruit; the fig tree and the vine yield their riches.... I will repay you for the years the locusts have eaten- the great locust and the young locust, the other locusts and the locust swarm- my great army that I sent among you. ... Then you will know that I am in Israel, that I am the LORD your God, and that there is no other; never again will my people be shamed.

Context: The prophet, Joel, has called the nation of Israel to repent of their sins and turn back to the Lord. Joel 2:12-27

Lessons and Truths:

1. To eliminate my fear, I need to constantly remember that God is great and has done great things.
2. The Lord wants me to experience His joy in my life.
3. The Lord wants me to be content where I am, looking around at His beauty and provisions.

4. I am to look around me for possibilities. God wants me to open my eyes and see things through His eyes.
5. His goodness produces fruit in my life for me to see.
6. God promises restoration for the repentant and faithful.

Prayer: Lord, help me to remember with a thankful heart the great things You have done in my life. Thank you for being a God who can and will restore me. I know You want me to live a joyful, productive life looking to You for all possibilities. Help me to see with Your eyes the many things around me that You have provided. Amen.

Well-Placed Fear: Joshua 4:24

He (God) did this so that all the peoples of the earth might know that the hand of the LORD is powerful and so that you might always fear the LORD your God.

How can I use these truths today?

What has God done for you that you need to thank Him for right now? _____

_____

_____

Where do you need His restoration?_____

_____

_____

Day 48-Zephaniah 3:16-17

God is Mighty to Save!

*O*n that day they will say to Jerusalem, "<u>Do not fear</u>, O Zion; do not let your hands hang limp. The LORD your God is with you, he is mighty to save. He will take great delight in you, he will quiet you with his love , he will rejoice over you with singing."

Context: Zephaniah was a prophet to Israel during King Josiah's reign. Although Josiah brought back worship of God and destroyed the idols, the people did not fully commit themselves to God. Zephaniah recounts their sins and promises hope for their future. Zephaniah 3:1-20

Lessons and Truths:

1. God does not want me paralyzed with fear so that even my limbs are not working.

2. God promises to: <u>be with me,</u> <u>save me</u> as He is mighty and greater than any enemy, <u>take delight in me</u> as He loves and cares for me, <u>quiet me with His love</u> as His love

always brings calmness, <u>rejoice over me with singing</u>.

3. God's very presence dispels fear.

Prayer: Lord, what wonderful promises You have made to me. Help me to count on Your presence, Your salvation, Your delight, Your love and Your joy to give my life meaning. Dispel any fears that might paralyze me. Thank you for Your promises and that You are indeed Almighty God! Amen.

Well-Placed Fear: Psalm 40:1-3

I waited patiently for the LORD; he turned to me and heard my cry. He lifted me out of the slimy pit, out of the mud and mire; he set my feet on a rock, he gave me a firm place to stand. He put a new song in my mouth, a hymn of praise to our God. Many will see and <u>fear </u>and put their trust in the LORD.

How can I use these truths today?

Which of the above promises can I apply to my life? _____

_____

_____

What fear am I facing that I need to trust Him to rescue me, place me on firm ground and give me a new song to sing?

_____

_____

_____

Day 49–Haggai 2:4–5

Fearlessly Work for God

'*But now be strong, O Zerubbabel,' declares the LORD. 'Be strong, O Joshua son of Jehozadak, the high priest. Be strong, all you people of the land,' declares the LORD, 'and work. For I am with you,' declares the LORD Almighty. This is what I covenanted with you when you came out of Egypt. And my Spirit remains among you. <u>Do not fear.</u>'*

Context: Haggai, a prophet of Israel, exhorted the people to get their priorities straight and make God number 1. He reminds them that by not putting God first, they are missing His blessings. Haggai 2:1-9

Lessons and Truths:

1.   God promises to be with me. His Holy Spirit never leaves me.
2.   God's Word is eternal and unchanging. He is the same yesterday, today and forever.
3.   His Holy Spirit dispels fear.

4. I am to put my mind to the tasks God has given me and not waste time and energy with fearful living.

5. God desires me to be strong, relying upon Him for my strength.

Prayer: Lord, help me to claim Your spirit within me and the power of You living with me. Give me the strength I need for today and keep my mind focused on You. Holy Spirit within me, bind my fears and give me victory. Thank you that you are unchanging and that I can rely upon You forever. Amen.

Well-Placed Fear: Psalm 90:11-12, 14

Who knows the power of your anger? For your wrath is as great as <u>the fear that is due you.</u> Teach us to number our days aright, that we may gain a heart of wisdom. ….… Satisfy us in the morning with your unfailing love, that we may sing for joy and be glad all our days.

How can I use these truths today?

What am I fearful of that will affect my living for God? _____

_____

_____

_____

Lord, bind these fears and help me to focus on living for you today. Amen

Day 50-Zechariah 8:13-17

Live for God

"*As* you have been an object of cursing among the nations, O Judah and Israel, so will I save you, and you will be a blessing. <u>Do not be afraid</u>, but let your hands be strong." This is what the LORD Almighty says: "Just as I had determined to bring disaster upon you and show no pity when your fathers angered me," says the LORD Almighty, "so now I have determined to do good again to Jerusalem and Judah. <u>Do not be afraid</u>. These are the things you are to do: Speak the truth to each other, and render true and sound judgment in your courts; do not plot evil against your neighbor, and do not love to swear falsely. I hate all this," declares the LORD.*

Context: Zechariah was a prophet in Israel after their return from the 70 years of captivity in Babylon. God exhorted them to trust Him and put past disastrous behaviors away and focus on godly actions. Zechariah 8:1-23

Lessons and Truths:

1. Living for God requires strength and courage.

2. God can and will save me and bless me.
3. God knows my past and the hardships I've endured.
4. God hates sinful behavior.
5. God admonishes me to live a godly life.
6. Acknowledging sin and turning to do what God desires brings blessings to me and those around me.

Prayer: Lord, forgive my sinfulness and help me to live worthy of Your calling. Help me to always speak truthfully to others, desire justice, avoid evil thoughts and deeds against others, and to not lie. I know You are calling me to a higher standard than what I find in the world. Fill me with Your Holy Spirit and grant me Your grace so that I might glorify You in my daily life. Amen.

Well-Placed Fear: Deuteronomy 4:9-10

Only be careful, and watch yourselves closely so that you do not forget the things your eyes have seen or let them slip from your heart as long as you live. Teach them to your children and to their children after them. Remember the day you stood before the LORD and your God at Horeb, when he said to me, "Assemble the people before me to hear my words so that they may learn to <u>revere (fear)</u> me as long as they live in the land and may teach them to their children.

How can I use these truths today?

What things does God want me to put away so I can serve him more fully? _____._____

_____

What do I need to tell someone that I know for certain about God? _____

Day 51-Malachi 3:2-5

Refiner's Fire

*B*ut *who can endure the day of his coming? Who can stand when he appears? For he will be like a refiner's fire or a launderer's soap. He will sit as a refiner and purifier of silver; he will purify the Levites and refine them like gold and silver. Then the LORD will have men who will bring offerings in righteousness, and the offerings of Judah and Jerusalem will be acceptable to the LORD, as in days gone by, as in former years. "So I will come near to you for judgment. I will be quick to testify against sorcerers, adulterers and perjurers, against those who defraud laborers of their wages, who oppress the widows and the father less, and deprive aliens of justice, but do not fear me," says the LORD Almighty.*

Context: Malachi was the last prophet before the birth of Christ. This passage looks forward to the end times, Christ's return and the judgment of unbelievers.

Malachi 2:17-3:5

Lessons and Truths:

1. The Lord will return to judge this sin-filled world.

2. No one is able to escape God's judgment.

3. God's judgment will be like a house cleaning – purifying out impurities and getting rid of those who live sin-filled lives.

4. God hates sin and He names specific sins – belief in sorcery and those who practice it, adulterers, liars, cheaters, thieves, oppressors, and those who thrive on injustice to others.

5. I do not need to fear judgment as I believe in Christ and have His Holy Spirit living within me. Christ's atoning blood cleanses me from sin and saves me from the judgment that sin brings.

Prayer: Lord, thank you for the power of Christ's blood to cleanse me from my sins and present me to You clean and spotless. I pray that I would take this coming judgment seriously and boldly speak about Christ' redemptive work on the cross to those I know who do not yet believe. Thank you for saving me and not giving me the punishment that my sins would deserve. You are indeed a merciful God. Amen.

Well-Placed Fear: Malachi 4:1-2

"Surely the day is coming; it will burn like a furnace. All the arrogant and every evildoer will be stubble, and that day that is coming will set them on fire," says the LORD Almighty. "Not a root or a branch will be left to them. But for you who <u>revere (fear)</u> my name, the sun of righteousness will arise with

healing in its wings. And you will go out and leap like calves released from the stall."

How can I use these truths today?

Where do I need to repent and turn to God?_____

_____

_____

What unbelievers do I know that need to be saved from judgment? _____

_____

_____

_____

Joseph Follows God

But after he had considered this, an angel of the LORD appeared to him in a dream and said, "Joseph son of David, do not be afraid to take Mary home as your wife, because what is conceived in her is from the Holy Spirit. She will give birth to a son, and you are to give him the name Jesus, because he will save his people from their sins.

When Joseph woke up, he did what the angel of the Lord had commanded him and took Mary home as his wife.

Context: God was reassuring Joseph that taking his fiancé, Mary, as his wife was the right thing to do. Custom dictated that he put her aside as she was unmarried and pregnant, but he knew he had not slept with her. Matthew 1:16-25

Lessons and Truths:
1. God knows the society in which I live and realizes that I need His encouragement and reassurance to do His will when in opposition to worldly standards.
2. God knows His will for my life.

3.   God has a plan of salvation for all mankind.
4.   Blessings come when I stay in God's will and do as He instructs.

Prayer: Lord, give me Your insight into the society in which You have placed me. Keep me in Your will in the midst of the sin that surrounds me. Help me to focus on You and the blessings that result in following Your will. Give me an urgency to witness to those that I know that do not know You as savior. Amen.

Well-Placed Fear: Jeremiah 32:40-41

I will make an everlasting covenant with them: I will never stop doing good to them, and <u>I will inspire them to fear me</u>, so that they will never turn away from me. I will rejoice in doing them good and will assuredly plant them in this land with all my heart and soul.

How can I use these truths today?

What good did God do for me yesterday? _____

_____

_____

Thank Him.

Whom do I know who does not know the Lord? _____

_____

_____

Pray for their salvation.

Day 53-Matthew 10:26-28 & Luke 12:2-5

Eternity at Stake

"*So do not be afraid of them. There is nothing concealed that will not be disclosed, or hidden that will not be made known. What I tell you in the dark, speak in the daylight; what is whispered in your ear, proclaim from the roofs. Do not be afraid of those who kill the body but cannot kill the soul. Rather, be afraid of the One who can destroy both soul and body in hell.*

Context: Jesus is giving words of caution and wisdom to the disciples as He prepares to send them out to tell others about Him and perform works in His name. Matthew 10:1-28 and Luke 12:1-5

Lessons and Truths:
1. God knows all truths both in the light and dark; nothing is hidden from Him.
2. Death of my body is not to be feared; my soul is eternal.
3. Only God can destroy both body and soul. He is the one to be feared.

4. God is to be feared (revered, awed, and trembled at) and not people, things or circumstances.
5. Hell is a place created by God for eternal punishment.

Prayer: Lord, You are the omnipotent, all-knowing God of the universe. You are the giver of life in both body and soul. Thank you that there is nothing or no one who can destroy my soul and keep me from eternity with You. Amen.

Well-Placed Fear: Matthew 10:28

Do not be afraid of those who kill the body but cannot kill the soul. Rather, <u>be afraid of the One</u> who can destroy both body and soul.

How can I use these truths today?

What fears of death and dying do I need to give to the Lord?

_____

_____

_____

Whom do I know who needs the good news of salvation because their unbelief puts them in jeopardy of going to hell for eternity?

_____

_____

_____

Pray for their salvation now!

Day 54–Matthew 10:29-31 & Luke 12:6-7

God Values Me

re not two sparrows sold for a penny? Yet not one of them will fall to the ground apart from the will of your Father. And even the very hairs of your head are all numbered. So don't be afraid; you are worth more than many sparrows.

Context: Prior to sending the disciples out to witness and perform miracles, Jesus instructs and reassures them of their great value to Him. Matthew 10:29-42 and Luke 12:6-12

Lessons and Truths:

1. God knows all there is to know about me – even how many hairs are on my head.
2. God values me above all the animals He created.
3. God's priority is man first, then the animals.
4. God, creator of the universe, places value on my life.
5. Since He cares, values and knows me, there should be no fear in my life.

Prayer: Lord, help me to cling to the knowledge that You love and value me above all else. Thank you for that incredible love and its power to dispel fear. Your love places me in your heart and on a firm foundation to face life's trials. Give me a 'no-fear' attitude today. Amen.

Well-Placed Fear: Isaiah 33:6

He will be the sure foundation for your times, a rich store of salvation and wisdom and knowledge: the fear of the LORD is the key to this treasure.

How can I use these truths today?

What fears do I have that need to be placed at his feet? _____

_____

_____

_____

What am I doing to increase my knowledge of God? _____

_____

_____

_____

Day 55-Matthew 14:25-31

Jesus Saves

*D*uring *the fourth watch of the night Jesus went out to them, walking on the lake. When the disciples saw him walking on the lake, they were terrified. "It's a ghost," they said, and cried out in fear. But Jesus immediately said to them: "Take courage! It is I. Don't be afraid." "Lord, if it's you," Peter replied, "tell me to come to you on the water." "Come," he said. Then Peter got down out of the boat, walked on the water and came toward Jesus. But when he saw the wind, he was afraid and, beginning to sink, cried out, "Lord, save me!" Immediately Jesus reached out his hand and caught him. "You of little faith," he said, "why did you doubt?"*

Context: After feeding 5,000 people, Jesus sent the disciples ahead across the Sea of Galilee while He dismissed the crowd. He then withdrew to have a quiet time of prayer. That evening, He went out to join them, walking on the water. Matthew 14:22-36

Lessons and Truths:

1. God's Word produces courage and increases faith.
2. God demands I keep my focus on Him for safety and salvation.
3. God's hand can and will catch me no matter where I find myself.
4. God's salvation, through Jesus, is immediate but requires that I reach out in faith.
5. Circumstances make room for doubt; God demands belief in Him for rescue.

Prayer: Lord, I desire to keep my focus upon You as You alone are the one who can bring me to safety. Help me to reach out to You through Jesus with increased faith. Allow Your Word to permeate my mind to produce courage. Give me a day filled with faith and assurance. Amen.

Well-Placed Fear: Psalm 145:18-20

The LORD is near to all who call on him, to all who call on him in truth. He fulfills the desires of those who fear him; he hears their cry and saves them. The LORD watches over all who love him, but all the wicked he will destroy.

How can I use these truths today?

Where am I doubting God that I need to reach out with faith?

_____

_____

_____

Do I know Jesus as my Savior? Do an assurance check today. Look up these verses.

<u>Admit need</u>: Romans 3:23, James 2:10

<u>Confess:</u> 1 John 1:8-10

<u>Believe:</u> John 5:24, John 14:6, Acts 2:22-24, 36 Romans 6:4

Day 56-Matthew 17:5-8

Being Up for Service

While he was still speaking, a bright cloud enveloped them, and a voice from the cloud said, "This is my Son, whom I love; with him I am well pleased. Listen to him!" When the disciples heard this, they fell facedown to the ground, terrified. But Jesus came and touched them. "Get up," he said. "<u>Don't be afraid</u>." When they looked up, they saw no one except Jesus.

Context: Jesus took Peter, James and John up on a high mountain where He met with Moses and Elijah. The disciples were overwhelmed with what they saw and heard. Matthew 17:1-13

Lessons and Truths:

1. Almighty God's presence produces awe, reverence and fear.
2. Being obedient involves listening to Jesus and doing as He directs.
3. Jesus wants me up and ready to serve, not face down in fear.

4.   When I'm fearful, focusing on Jesus alone will restore me.

Prayer: Lord, give me a heart that is responsive to Jesus' leading so that I may please You with my deeds and actions. Help me to remember to focus upon Jesus when I am experiencing doubts and fear. Amen.

Well-Placed Fear: Joshua 24:14-15

"*Now fear the LORD and serve him with all faithfulness. Throw away the gods your forefathers worshiped beyond the River and in Egypt, and serve the LORD. But if serving the LORD seems undesirable to you, then choose for yourselves this day whom you will serve, whether the gods your forefathers served beyond the river, or the gods of the Amorites, in whose land you are living. But as for me and my house hold, we will serve the LORD.*"

How can I use these truths today?

Am I serving God or idols (money, career, materialism, etc)?

_____

_____

_____

Where does God want me to serve him wholeheartedly?

_____

_____

_____

Day 57-Matthew 28:5-10

Joyful Reunion

The angel said to the women, "Do not be afraid, for I know that you are looking for Jesus, who was crucified. He is not here; he has risen, just as he said. Come and see the place where he lay. Then go quickly and tell his disciples: 'He has risen from the dead and is going ahead of you into Galilee. There you will see him.' Now I have told you." So the women hurried away from the tomb, afraid yet filled with joy, and ran to tell his disciples. Suddenly Jesus met them. "Greetings," he said. They came to him, clasped his feet and worshiped him. Then Jesus said to them, "Do not be afraid. Go and tell my brothers to go to Galilee; there they will see me."

Context: The women visited the tomb of Jesus intending to anoint His body with spices. When they arrived, there was an earthquake and the stone covering the tomb was rolled away. The guards were paralyzed with fear as an angel sat upon the stone. He told the women that Jesus was not in the tomb as He had risen. Matthew 28:1-10

Lessons and Truths:

1. In God's presence, our immediate response is fear.
2. God seeks to comfort me when I'm afraid. He knows my mind, heart and emotions.
3. The *result* of an encounter with Jesus is joy!
4. Jesus addressed the women personally. He knows me personally, too.
5. My response to meeting Jesus personally should be to go and tell others about Him.
6. I worship a living LORD and not an empty tomb.

Prayer: Lord Jesus, make me quick to tell others about You and Your saving work on the cross. You are indeed living and can actively comfort me. Help me to keep my focus on You and not the emptiness of this world that surrounds me. Replace my fear with joy as You did for the women. Amen.

Well-Placed Fear: Psalm 115:12-13

The LORD remembers us and will bless us: He will bless the house of Israel, he will bless the house of Aaron,   <u>he will bless those who fear the LORD</u>---small and great alike.

How can I use these truths today?

Whom do I know who needs to hear about Jesus? _____

_____

Where do I need God to replace my fears with joy? _____

_____

_____

Day 58-Mark 5:21-24a, 35- 36 & Luke 8:40-42,49-50

Faith Required

When Jesus had again crossed over by boat to the other side of the lake, a large crowd gathered around him while he was by the lake. Then one of the synagogue rulers, named Jairus, came there. Seeing Jesus, he fell at his feet and pleaded earnestly with him, "My little daughter is dying. Please come and put your hands on her so that she will be healed and live." So Jesus went with him. …. While Jesus was still speaking, some men came from the house of Jairus, the synagogue ruler. "Your daughter is dead," they said. "Why bother the teacher anymore?" Ignoring what they said, Jesus told the synagogue ruler, "Don't be afraid; just believe."

Context: Jairus, the synagogue ruler, asked Jesus to come heal his sick daughter. On the way to his home, Jesus was delayed by the needy crowd, and Jairus received word his daughter had died. Mark 5:21-43

Lessons and Truths:

1. Trusting Jesus requires ignoring things that would make

me doubt Him and stand firm.

2. Fear is a result of doubt and unbelief.

3. Believing his daughter still lived required much faith, likewise Jesus requires that level of faith from me, too.

4. Going to Jesus for help always produces results.

Prayer: Lord, I am in need of extra faith. I know that my fears come from doubting You and Your ability to help, guide, protect and be with me. Give me assurance through Your Word and indwelling Holy Spirit to conquer my fears and stand firm in You. Amen.

Well-Placed Fear: Hebrews 11:1 and Proverbs 1:7

11:1 Now faith is being sure of what we hope for and certain of what we do not see.

1:7 The fear of the LORD is the beginning of knowledge, but fools despise wisdom and discipline.

How can I use these truths today?

Where am I being tempted to doubt God? _____

_____

_____

_____

Ask God to be able to stand firm in this situation and fill you with faith, John 16: 24 *Until now you have not asked for anything in my name. Ask and you will receive, and your joy will be complete.*

Day 59-Luke 1:11-14

God's Answer Brings Joy

Then an angel of the Lord appeared to him, standing at the right side of the altar of incense. When Zechariah saw him, he was startled and gripped with fear. But the angel said to him: "Do not be afraid, *Zechariah; your prayer has been heard. Your wife Elizabeth will bear you a son, and you are to give him the name John. He will be a joy and delight to you, and many will rejoice because of his birth.*

Context: Zechariah had a visit from the angel Gabriel while serving in the temple. He told Zachariah that his barren wife Elizabeth would have a child, and they were to name him John. Zechariah doubted Gabriel's words and lost the ability to speak until John was born. Luke 1:5-25, 57-66

Lessons and Truths:

1. God is accessible.
2. God knows the desires of my heart and hears my prayers.
3. I need to seek God in prayer diligently and ask him for those things that mean so much to me.

4.   God's answer to my prayers results in joy and delight. God's answers to my prayers affect many for good.

Prayer: Lord, give me perseverance in prayer to wait for Your timing and Your answers with hope. You promise to never disappoint if I hope in You. (Isaiah 49: 23b) Thank you that You are accessible and that You hear my prayers. Amen.

Well-Placed Fear: Psalm 119:74

May those who fear you rejoice when they see me, for I have put my hope in your word.

How can I use these truths today?

What do I desire from God above all else?_____

_____

_____

How has God answered me in the past and what joy did I receive?

_____

_____

_____

Remembering God's blessings in the past gives me hope for the future.

Day 60-Luke 1:29-34, 38

Mary's Courage

*M*ary *was greatly troubled at his words and wondered what kind of greeting this might be. But the angel said to her, "Do not be afraid, Mary, you have found favor with God. You will be with child and give birth to a son, and you are to give him the name Jesus. He will be great and will be called the Son of the Most High. The Lord God will give him the throne of his father David, and he will reign over the house of Jacob forever; his kingdom will never end." "I am the Lord's servant," Mary answered. "May it be to me as you have said." Then the angel left her.*

Context: Mary, a young virgin, was visited by the angel Gabriel who told her that she was to bear the Son of God. She was overwhelmed and frightened, but she showed great courage and stated that she was God's servant. Luke 1:26-38

Lessons and Truths:

1.   God knows me by name.

2. God has a purpose for my future that involves working for Him.

3. God can and does show me favor.

4. My response to God needs to be one of obedience.

5. Blessings come from being obedient to God's call.

Prayer: Lord, I would love to be like Mary. Help me to be obedient to Your call and willing to do that which would bring glory to You. Help me to put my fears aside and focus on serving You. I am overwhelmed that You know my name and have a special work and place for me to serve You. Amen.

Well-Placed Fear: Luke 1:49-50

for the Mighty One has done great things for me- holy is his name. His mercy extends to those who fear him, from generation to generation.

How can I use these truths today?

Where do I need to be obedient?_____

_____

_____

In what circumstances do I especially need God's mercy?

_____

_____

_____

Day 61-Luke 2:8-12

Good News Arrives

*A*nd there were shepherds living out in the fields *nearby, keeping watch over their flocks at night. An angel of the Lord appeared to them, and the glory of the Lord shone around them, and they were terrified. But the angel said to them, "Do not be afraid. I bring you good news of great joy that will be for all the people. Today in the town of David a Savior has been born to you; he is Christ the Lord. This will be a sign to you: You will find a baby wrapped in cloths and lying in a manger."*

Context: Shepherds received the news of Jesus' birth in a glorious manner. Luke 2:8-20

Lessons and Truths:

1. God's plan of redemption is good news to you and me.
2. Salvation brings joy and is open to all people.
3. God's good news came in the form of a baby, humble in birth.
4. Christ the Lord was born to save you and me.

Prayer: Lord, I am so unworthy of the great gift You gave us in Your son. Your plan to redeem me is good news indeed and brings me great joy. Thank you for choosing me and making a plan to save me. Help me to share the joy of my salvation with someone today. Amen.

Well-Placed Fear: Psalm 102:15-16

The nations will <u>fear the name of the LORD</u>, all the kings of the earth will <u>revere (fear)</u> your glory. For the LORD will rebuild Zion and appear in his glory.

How can I use these truths today?

What joy has God given me in this study that I can share?

_____

_____

_____

Whom do I know who needs to hear the good news about Jesus?

_____

_____

_____

Day 62-Luke 5:5-11

Going Fishing

Simon answered, "Master, we've worked hard all night and haven't caught anything. But because you say so, I will let down the nets." When they had done so, they caught such a large number of fish that their nets began to break. So they signaled their partners in the other boat to come and help them, and they came and filled both boats so full that they began to sink. When Simon Peter saw this, he fell at Jesus' knees and said, "Go away from me, Lord; I am a sinful man!" For he and all his companions were astonished at the catch of fish they had taken, and so were James and John, the sons of Zebedee, Simon's partners. Then Jesus said to Simon, "Don't be afraid; from now on you will catch men." So they pulled their boats up on shore, left everything and followed him.

Context: Jesus met his future disciples after a futile night of fishing. They saw his provision and power, and they responded to his calling with out fear. Luke 5:1-11

Lessons and Truths:

1. God wants me to experience His power in my life and not be afraid.
2. God has a purpose for each person to fulfill.
3. God's will is affirmative; you will catch men! No doubting allowed.
4. God's will can not be thwarted; no one can change it.
5. God's plan leads to action and full commitment to Him.

Prayer: Lord, open my eyes so that I can see, feel, and be touched by Your power. Take away my doubts and fears so that I can live in the assurance of Your will for my life. I know You have a plan for me so help me to be focused and relying on You for my pathway. Amen.

Well-Placed Fear: Luke 5:26

Everyone was amazed and gave praise to God. They were filled with <u>awe (fear)</u> and said, "We have seen remarkable things today."

How can I use these truths today?

Where do I need to praise God for the amazing things He has done and is doing in my life? _____

_____

_____

Where do I need to claim God's affirmation? No doubt or fear, God will accomplish this in my life!_____

_____

Day 63-Luke 12:32-34

Treasured Living

"*Do not be afraid, little flock, for your Father has been pleased to give you the kingdom. Sell your possessions and give to the poor. Provide purses for yourselves that will not wear out, a treasure in heaven that will not be exhausted, where no thief comes near and no moth destroys. For where your treasure is, there your heart will be also.*"

Context: Jesus is addressing his disciples with warnings and encouragements, teaching them godly principles of living. Luke 12:22-34

Lessons and Truths:

1. God claims me as His child.
2. God delights in giving me the kingdom which includes salvation, eternal life, His righteousness, His spirit to indwell me, and His peace.
3. The treasures God has for me are inexhaustible; they are beyond the reach of any person or thing to destroy them.
4. God's treasures will also keep hold of my heart.

Prayer: Lord, Your treasures for me are unfathomable. Thank you for Your promise that they cannot be destroyed or touched, and that You will hold my heart. Lord, help me to trust You fully with my heart so that I can access all the treasures You have in store for me. Open them to me and give me courage to live each day to the fullest. Amen.

Well-Placed Fear: Proverbs 10:27

The fear of the LORD adds length to life, but the years of the wicked are cut short.

How can I use these truths today?

What treasures can I thank God for today?_____

_____

_____

Take one of the treasures _____ and claim it right now.

Day 64-John 12:14-16

A Donkey Ride

*J*esus *found a young donkey and sat upon it, as it is written, "Do not be afraid, O Daughter of Zion; see, your king is coming, seated on a donkey's colt." At first his disciples did not understand all this. Only after Jesus was glorified did they realize that these things had been written about him and that they had done these things to him.*

Context: Jesus is quoting from Zechariah 9: 9 which prophesized that the king-messiah would enter Jerusalem seated on a donkey. The crowd greeted him with palm branches and shouts. John 12:12-19

Lessons and Truths:

1.   God keeps his promises. He told the people through the prophet Zechariah between 520 B.C. and 480 B.C that Messiah would come and enter Jerusalem seated on a donkey. Zechariah 9: 9. This event recorded by John fulfilled this ancient prophecy.

2.   God wants me to rejoice with Him and not fear the future.

3.   God opens my mind to understand Him more fully when I know the glorified Jesus and have the Holy Spirit dwelling within me.

Prayer: Lord, I am so thankful that You keep Your promises. What Your Word foretold about You came about just as You said. I praise You for your omniscience and sovereignty. Help me to know You more fully and live with Your Spirit indwelling and guiding me today. Empower me to follow You more closely and trust You more completely. Amen.

Well-Placed Fear: Psalm 119:79-80

May those <u>who fear you</u> turn to me, those who understand your statutes. May my heart be blameless toward your decrees, that I may not be put to shame.

How can I use these truths today?

Seek God's understanding of these promises:

Philippians 4:13: I can do everything through him who gives me strength.

I Thessalonians 5:24: The one who calls you is faithful and he will do it.

How can you claim them today?_____

_____

_____

_____

Day 65–John 14:27

Peaceful Living

eace I leave with you; my peace I give to you. I do not give to you as the world gives. <u>Do not let you hearts be troubled</u> and <u>do not be afraid</u>.

<u>Context:</u> Jesus knew His time on earth was ending. He spoke lovingly with His disciples about many subjects, showing His mercy and compassion for them. He knew the words would bring comfort to them in the days, months and years ahead. John 14:23-27

<u>Lessons and Truths:</u>
1. Peace comes from God.
2. God's peace is freely given and has no worldly strings attached.
3. God's peace can not be bought; it is priceless.
4. God's peace comforts me at the very core of my being, my heart. His peace calms my emotions, desires and fears.

Prayer: Lord, grant me Your peace each day so that I may serve You. I know Your peace will calm me and keep fears, desires and conflicting emotions away. Thank you for such a wonderful gift that You give so freely. Help me to hold on to Your peace throughout the day. Amen.

Well-Placed Fear: Proverbs 3:5-8

Trust in the LORD with all your heart and lean not on your own understanding; in all your ways acknowledge him, and he will make your paths straight. Do not be wise in your own eyes; <u>fear the LORD</u> and shun evil. This will bring health to your body and nourishment to your bones.

How can I use these truths today?

Where do I need to trust God to bring His peace to me?

_____

_____

_____

What part of me needs His peace – my heart, emotions, desires, fears?_____

_____

_____

Day 66-Acts 18 9-11

Keep on Witnessing

One night the Lord spoke to Paul in a vision: "<u>Do not be afraid</u>; keep on speaking, do not be silent. For I am with you, and no one is going to attack and harm you, because I have many people in this city." So Paul stayed for a year and a half, teaching them the word of God.

Context: Paul had been preaching to the Jews in Corinth. They opposed Paul and became abusive. God appeared to Paul in a vision telling him to stay and continue preaching and teaching the Gentiles. Acts 18:1-17

Lessons and Truths:
1. God speaks to me personally; I matter to Him.
2. The good news of the Gospel of Christ will be spoken. It cannot be stopped by opposition.
3. God knows my fears about witnessing. He promises to always be with me.
4. God has many resources that I am not aware of both in heaven and on earth.

5.   Doing God's work requires time, persistence and courage.

Prayer: Lord, thank you for personally speaking to me through Your Word. Give me courage to witness for You, telling others about Jesus and His redeeming work. Help me to see and use the resources You provide with a grateful heart. Give me diligence in doing Your work. Amen.

Well-Placed Fear: Psalm 119:57-58 and 63-64

You are my portion, O LORD; I have promised to obey your words. I have sought your face with all my heart; be gracious to me according to your promise. ....
I am a friend to all who <u>*fear*</u> *you, to all who follow your precepts. The earth is filled with your love, O LORD; teach me your decrees.*

How can I use the truths today?

Who am I afraid to witness to and why?_____

_____

What resources do I need to be able to witness to this person? (Be specific) _____

_____

_____

Right now, where does God want me to be persistent and show courage in serving Him?_____

_____

_____

Blessings Around

After the men had gone a long time without food, Paul stood up before them and said: "Men, you should have taken my advice not to sail from Crete: then you would have spared yourselves this damage and loss. But now I urge you to keep up your courage, because not one of you will be lost; only the ship will be destroyed. Last night an angel of the God whose I am and whom I serve stood beside me and said, 'Do not be afraid, Paul. You must stand trial before Caesar; and God has graciously given you the lives of all who sail with you.' So keep up your courage, men, for I have faith in God that it will happen just as he told me. Nevertheless, we must run aground on some island."

Context: Paul was a prisoner on his way to Rome to stand trial before Caesar. He was in chains and under guard. They were caught in a storm on the Mediterranean Sea and their ship was in jeopardy of sinking. Acts 27:13-44

Lessons and Truths:

1. God gives encouragement to me when I need it most.
2. When God blesses me, it affects Christian and non-Christians around me.
3. God knows the plans He has for me; I am secure in Him.
4. Courage comes from Jesus.

Prayer: Lord, help me to trust solely in You for my life and all the circumstances that surround me. I thank you ahead of time for the blessings You will bring into my life that will affect me and those who surround me. Help me to be an encouragement to others today reflecting Your love and provision. Amen.

Well-Placed Fear: Deuteronomy 10:12-13, 21

And now, O Israel, what does the LORD your God ask of you but to fear the LORD your God, to walk in all his ways, to love him, to serve the LORD your God with all your heart and with all your soul, and to observe the LORD's commands and decrees that I am giving you today for your own good?.... He is your praise; he is your God, who performed for you those great and awesome wonders you saw with your own eyes.

How can I use these truths today?

As a believer, who can I encourage today?_____

_____

What can I do to show that I am walking in His ways, loving and serving Him?_____

_____

Day 68–1 Peter 3:13–15a

Hope-Filled Living

Who is going to harm you if you are eager to do good? But even if you should suffer for what is right, you are blessed. "Do not fear what they fear; do not to be frightened." But in your hearts set apart Christ as Lord. Always be prepared to give an answer to everyone who asks you to give the reason for the hope that you have.

Context: Peter is writing to encourage Christians to live fearlessly, being Christ-like examples in the world. 1 Peter 3:8-22

Lessons and Truths:

1. Suffering brings blessings.
2. I am not to fear the world around me as unbelievers do.
3. Christ is to be LORD of my life.
4. Faith in Christ gives hope to my life.
5. God expects me to testify to the hope I have in Christ (my salvation).

Prayer: Lord, help me to see suffering and trials as opportunities for blessing. Let my testimony be bold about the hope You have given me in Christ. Cover my fears with an extra portion of faith and give me someone today to tell about You. Amen.

Well-Placed Fear: Psalm 49:5,15

Why should I _fear_ when evil days come, when wicked deceivers surround me-

But God will redeem my life from the grave; he will surely take me to himself. Selah

How can I use these truths today?

What blessings do I see from my current suffering? _____

_____

_____

Who can I tell about the hope that I have in Christ?_____

_____

_____

Day 69-Revelation 1:17-18

First and Last

When I saw him, I fell at his feet as though dead. Then he placed his right hand on me and said: "Do not be afraid. I am the First and the Last. I am the Living One; I was dead, and behold I am alive for ever and ever! And I hold the keys of death and Hades."

Context: The disciple John had a vision while exiled on the isle of Patmos. Jesus appeared to him and told him to write down what He was going to show him and send it to seven specific churches in Asia Minor. Revelation 1:9-20

Lessons and Truths:
1. Being in the presence of God is overwhelming and would cause anyone to fear.
2. Jesus was with God in the beginning (First) and will be there when all things end (Last).
3. Jesus is alive – the Living One!
4. Jesus is eternal – forever and ever!

5. Jesus' presence gives me assurance and hope so I don't have to fear.
6. Jesus is in control of life and death.

Prayer: Lord, may I give all my fears to You and let Your spirit comfort me, dispelling all my doubts and troubling thoughts. Help me to know without a doubt that You are eternal and living, and that You do control all things – even life and death. Place Your hand upon me and give me Your assurance and peace today. Amen.

Well-Placed Fear: Hebrews 12:28-29

Therefore, since we are receiving a kingdom that cannot be shaken, let us be thankful, and so worship God acceptably <u>with reverence and awe (fear)</u>, for our "God is a consuming fire".

How can I use these truths today?

What can you thank God for? _____

_____

_____

What fears do you have that you need Him to touch and replace with peace and hope? _____

_____

_____

Day 70-Revelation 2:9-10

Crown of Life

" *I* know your afflictions and your poverty—yet you are rich! I know the slander of those who say they are Jews and are not, but are a synagogue of Satan. *Do not be afraid* of what you are about to suffer. I tell you, the devil will put some of you in prison to test you, and you will suffer persecution for ten days. Be faithful, even to the point of death, and I will give you the crown of life."

Context: In John's vision, specific messages were given to the early churches. This was part of the message to the church in Smyrna. The warnings and encouragements were ones that could be applied to churches today. Revelation 2:8-11

Lessons and Truths:

1. God knows my circumstances intimately and wants to remind me how rich I am in knowing Him! Keep a God-focus, not a problem-focus.

2. God's plan for my life often requires me to endure difficult times.

3. God promises to be faithful.

4. Suffering due to persecution has a time limit to it.

5. If death is required in persecution, He promises to be faithful and reward me with eternal blessings, a crown of life.

Prayer: Lord, You know the ins and outs of my life. You see what makes me struggle and causes me grief. Help me to count as joy any persecution I am facing for Your sake. Remind me of Your faithfulness and Your eternal rewards. Cause me to fix my gaze upon You alone. Amen.

Well-Placed Fear: Revelation 19:5-6

Then a voice came from the throne, saying: "Praise our God all you his servants, you who <u>fear </u>him, both small and great!" Then I heard what sounded like a great multitude, like the roar of rushing waters and like loud peals of thunder, shouting: "Hallelujah! For our Lord God Almighty reigns".

How can I use these truths today?

What problems am I facing that I need to keep a God-focus not a problem-focus?_____

_____

_____

God is sovereign, holy and worthy of all my praise. What can I praise Him for specifically today? _____

_____

_____

Author's Note

Thank you for coming on this journey with me through the Bible. I pray that you have grown closer in your walk with the LORD and have established a habit of daily Bible study. I also pray that you are more aware of God and His character, realizing what Scripture teaches us about Him!

I noticed as I did this study that there were many more references to "Do Not Fear" in the Old Testament than in the Gospels of the New Testament when Jesus was on Earth. Very few references occur after Pentecost and the arrival of the Holy Spirit. The indwelling of the Holy Spirit allows us to have God with us at all times. We can pray and receive strength immediately and power to overcome those things that cause us fear.

The question is why don't we do that regularly? I think it is our lack of faith in God's character and not knowing Him well enough. I pray that you know God more fully and intimately now and can continue to walk with less fear and more assurance that God is with you at all times.

I have included five more days that focus on courage, and what we can count on since we know God. He has given us assurances in His Word that we can keep close and receive definite encouragement.

Blessings,

Linda Knight

<u>Day 71-Romans 8:37-39</u>

No Separation

No, in all these things we are more than conquerors through him who loved us. For I am convinced that neither death nor life, neither angels nor demons, neither the present nor the future, nor any powers, neither height nor depth, nor anything else in all creation, will be able to separate us from the love of God that is in Christ Jesus our Lord.

<u>Context:</u> Paul's letter to the Roman Christians was intended to strengthen, encourage and confirm them in their faith. Romans 8:28-39

<u>Lessons and Truths:</u>

1. God's ultimate love was sending Christ to reconcile me to Him.
2. Through God's love I can be a conqueror in all aspects of my life.
3. Angels and demons are real.
4. God is timeless knowing both past, present and future.

5. Nothing physical or spiritual is more powerful than God's love.
6. God's love through Christ creates an inseparable bond between God and me.

Prayer: Lord, You are greater than any foe or circumstance I that will ever face. Help me to trust You more fully in all aspects of my life and surrender my life to You through Your son, Jesus. Bind me to You through Christ that I may feel that bond of love each day as I endeavor to live for You. Amen.

How can I use these truths today?

God is greater than _____

_____ that I will face today!

How can I show God's love to others? (Be specific.)

_____

_____

_____

_____

Justification by Faith

But what does it say? "The word is near you; it is in your mouth and in your heart," that is, the word of faith we are proclaiming: That if you confess with your mouth, "Jesus is Lord," and believe in your heart that God raised him from the dead, you will be saved. For it is with your heart that you believe and are justified, and it is with your mouth that you confess and are saved. As the Scripture says, "Any one who trusts in him will never be put to shame," For there is no difference between Jew and Gentile-the same Lord is Lord of all and richly blesses all who call on him, for, "Everyone who calls on the name of the Lord will be saved."

Context: Paul is writing to the Roman Christians to reaffirm their confession of faith in Christ as Savior. Romans 10:1-15

Lessons and Truths:
1. Salvation requires faith in Jesus and His resurrection.
2. Faith believes Jesus is alive.

3. Faith brings justification, a position of right relationship to God.
4. Trust in God frees me from condemnation.
5. God is Lord of all mankind.
6. One needs to call on the Lord for salvation.
7. God will answer the believer's call.

Prayer: Lord, thank you for Your perfect plan to save me and bring me into a close relationship. Faith in You frees me to live for You boldly. Continue to bring me to deeper faith and contentment in You. Fill me with assurance that I am indeed saved and cherished by You. Amen.

How can I use these truths today?

Whom do I know who needs to know Jesus and be saved?

_____

Pray for them right now.

What can I do to keep on growing in my faith? _____

_____

_____

Research Bible studies available at your church or in your community. Go online and look at websites for Bible Study Fellowship, www.biblestudyfellowship.org or Community Bible Studies, www.communitybiblestudy.org, and see if there are classes in your local community. Both of these are interdenominational Bible-based studies.

Day 73–Ephesians 2:4-10

God's Grace in Action

But because of his great love for us, God, who is rich in mercy, made us alive with Christ even when we were dead in transgressions—it is by grace you have been saved. And God raised us up with Christ and seated us with him in the heavenly realms in Christ Jesus, in order that in the coming ages he might show the incomparable riches of his grace, expressed in his kindness to us in Christ Jesus. For it is by grace you have been saved, through faith—and this not from yourselves, it is the gift of God – not by works, so that no one can boast. For we are God's workmanship, created in Christ Jesus to do good works, which God prepared in advance for us to do.

Context: Paul was writing to encourage the believers in Ephesus by explaining more fully God's mercy and grace. Ephesians 2:1-10

Lessons and Truths:

1.   God is merciful and loving.
2.   God saved me through Christ's sacrifice on the cross.

3. Sin equals death and separation from God.

4. I am saved and sealed by my faith in Christ for eternity.

5. Grace equals unmerited favor from God. I received this grace from God when I put my faith in Jesus

6. Nothing I can do myself can earn me salvation. Nothing I can do will erase my sin.

7. God is at work in me and will use me to do good works for Him.

Prayer: Lord, You are indeed merciful and loving to send Jesus to save me from the punishment of death that my sins would deserve. Thank you for Your grace and mercy. Use me to do Your good work and to let others know of Your bountiful grace. Amen.

How can I use these truths today?

Who can I show God's mercy and grace to today?_____

_____

_____

What work would God have me do or does He have me doing already for Him? _____

_____

_____

Godly Armor

Finally, be strong in the Lord and in his mighty power. Put on the full armor of God so that you can take your stand against the devil's schemes. For our struggle is not against flesh and blood, but against the rulers, against the authorities, against the powers of this dark world and against the spiritual forces of evil in the heavenly realms. Therefore put on the full armor of God, so that when the day of evil comes, you may be able to stand your ground, and after you have done everything, to stand.

Context: Paul writes to the Ephesians with practical thoughts for standing firm in the faith. Ephesians 6:10-20

Lessons and Truths:
1.   God is powerful and mighty.
2.   I can count on God's power and strength in my battles.
3.   The devil schemes to try and defeat me.
4.   Evil forces are at war with God both here on Earth and in the heavenly realm.

5.   God's armor will protect me.

6.   I need to stand firm in the Lord.

Prayer: Father God, You are mighty and more powerful than any force here on earth or in heaven. Thank you that Your armor will protect me against Satan's attack. Help me to stand firm for You, grounded in Your Word. Amen.

How can I use these truths today?

What satanic attack am I facing, right now, that is trying to take my focus off God? _____

_____

_____

What godly armor will I use today? Prayer, God's Word, truth, the Gospel, faith? _____

_____

_____

Day 75-Hebrews 11:1-3 & 6

Faith for Living

Now faith is being sure of what we hope for and certain of what we do not see. This is what the ancients were commended for. By faith we understand that the universe was formed at God's command, so that what is seen was not made out of what was visible.

And without faith it is impossible to please God, because anyone who comes to him must believe that he exists and that he rewards those who earnestly seek him.

Context: Hebrews has no stated author but it is believed to have been written by Paul. It is a letter to Jewish believers as they struggled with leaving Judaism and embracing the freedom in Christ. This chapter tells of many in the Bible who lived by faith as examples for us to follow. Hebrews 11:1-40

Lessons and Truths:

1. Faith requires belief and hope in the invisible God.
2. Understanding creation requires faith.
3. God created all there is out of nothing.

4. God existed before creation.
5. Faith pleases God.
6. Faith means believing in God and His ability to reward me.

Prayer: Lord, You are creator of all and are greater than all of Your creation. You are eternal and sovereign over all of Your creation. I know that faith pleases You. Help me to step out in greater faith today and trust You in each encounter I have. Amen.

How can I use these truths today?

Where in my life do I need to exercise more faith? _____

_____

_____

What specific problems am I facing today where I need an extra measure of faith?_____

_____

_____

How is my faith stronger since I have completed this study?

_____

_____

_____

**Need
additional
copies?**

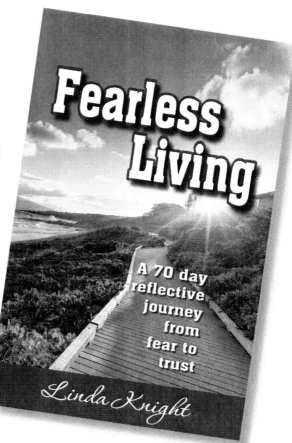

To order more copies of
Fearless Living,

contact NewBookPublishing.com

❏   Order online at:
     NewBookPublishing.com/bookstore

❏   Call 877-311-5100 or

❏   Email Info@NewBookPublishing.com